NEW YORK DOZEN

Michael J. Crosbie

Gen X Architects

images

Published in Australia in 2011 by
The Images Publishing Group Pty Ltd
ABN 89 059 734 431
6 Bastow Place, Mulgrave, Victoria 3170, Australia
Tel: +61 3 9561 5544 Fax: +61 3 9561 4860
books@imagespublishing.com
www.imagespublishing.com

Copyright © The Images Publishing Group Pty Ltd 2011
The Images Publishing Group Reference Number: 919

National Library of Australia Cataloguing-in-Publication entry:

Author:	Crosbie, Michael J. (Michael James)
Title:	New York dozen : Gen X architects / Michael J. Crosbie.
ISBN:	9781864703962 (hbk.)
Subjects:	Architecture—New York—New York.
	Architects—New York—New York.
Dewey Number:	720.97471

Additional photography courtesy Damian Wood

Coordinating editor: Beth Browne

Production by The Graphic Image Studio Pty Ltd, Mulgrave, Australia
www.tgis.com.au

Pre-publishing services by United Graphic Pte Ltd, Singapore

Printed on 140 gsm GoldEast Matt Art by Everbest Printing Co. Ltd., in Hong Kong/China

IMAGES has included on its website a page for special notices in relation to this and its other
publications. Please visit www.imagespublishing.com.

New York City is nothing if not a magnet for high aspirations, lofty dreams, and big plans. For generations, fine design talents from here and everywhere have hit the city's streets running—but not all are able to leap the potholes of extremely volatile market forces, learn well the down-to-earth realities of running a business, and land on their feet with a sense of joy and accomplishment.

The city is in a very particular place and time. Government agencies, developers, and the citizenry have never been more actively involved (most times collaboratively) in city building that is economically, environmentally, and socially sustainable. I believe 9/11 and the growing awareness of what climate change could do to our streets and shorelines have had much to do with it. So has a tough economy. Unprecedented public/private partnerships and a few enlightened developers are, as never before, allowing younger firms to get their foot in the door of some of the city's most exciting projects. At the same time, an ever-more-connected world is giving them previously unheard of opportunities beyond local borders, which this generation seems more than ready—and able—to take on.

My friend Mike Crosbie set a daunting task for himself: select 12 young New York City-based firms that epitomize this new generation of architects and designers. It could not have been easy.

What makes these Young Turks different from previous generations? The vocabulary hasn't changed all that much, but the definitions have. "Collaboration" still means teaming, but now teams cross ever-wider disciplines. "Cross-disciplinary" is much more than an architect designing a line of furniture or accessories (though that is still very much a part of it). This generation of designers is taking the lead in hands-on exploration of new materials and fabrication methods, using technology to the nth degree—but not only to create the iconic or the fantastical.

It is a tribute to the 12 firms presented here—who represent so many more—that they have taken that leap of faith, especially in these times, when young firms and their more seasoned counterparts are facing the new and unexpected challenges of this century—along with existing challenges from the last century. Besides dealing with day-to-day practicalities to ensure their businesses survive and thrive, these firms bring a heightened sense of advocacy to their practices, where environmental and social responsibility have become a natural part of their lexicon.

As a New York-based journalist for 20-plus years, the last 10 as editor of ArchNewsNow.com and *Oculus* magazine, the American Institute of Architects New York Chapter's quarterly journal, I have seen my fair share of rising young architect stars. Many have soared to become leading talents on an international stage. Sadly, so many more have crashed and burned—but not for lack of trying.

The spring 2004 issue of *Oculus,* themed "New York Next: Faces of the Future," profiled several firms included in this book, so I re-read the issue to see what might be different in just seven years. Among the words used most often by designers surveyed in 2004: optimism, imagination, dreams, simplicity. Among the words used most often by designers presented here: research, fabrication, clarity, cross-disciplinary, pragmatism. A sign of the times?

I am pleased to call many of the New York Dozen my friends, and delighted to see them recognized in these pages. Their dedication, skill, and, dare I say, pragmatic optimism will take them far. This book is a time capsule, and it will be interesting to revisit it 7, 15, and 25 years from now to see just where that pragmatic optimism finds them.

—Kristen Richards, Hon. AIA, Hon. ASLA

This book was inspired by another book. Published nearly 40 years ago, *Five Architects* was the first self-promotional publication to appear in a new age of media attention to architecture. It continues to be a touchstone in the debate about the nature of architectural fame. *Five Architects* prompted this new assessment of young architects who are working in New York, making their mark in very different ways from their five counterparts in the late 1960s and early '70s. This new book is also indebted to that landmark publication by bringing young architects together within one volume where they speak about their own work, their architectural values, and how much the world of architecture has changed since *Five Architects*.

Five Architects presented the work of Peter Eisenman, Michael Graves, Charles Gwathmey, John Hejduk, and Richard Meier—architects then in their late 30s and early 40s who had yet to achieve superstardom, but who were on a trajectory towards it. All five had studied architecture at elite schools: Eisenman and Meier at Cornell, Gwathmey at Yale, and Hejduk and Graves at Harvard. All five were working in and around New York and were teaching

at architecture schools in the vicinity: Princeton, Yale, Cooper Union. A "New York School," or even a group known as the "New York Five" was not their invention; the "New York Five" moniker was coined by Paul Goldberger, then the *New York Times* architecture critic. The book included projects by each of the five architects, an introduction by architectural theorist and historian Colin Rowe, and commentary by architectural historian and critic Kenneth Frampton.

The idea for such a book grew out of closed sessions held at the Museum of Modern Art (MoMA) in the late 1960s, hosted by Arthur Drexler, then the director of MoMA's Department of Architecture and Design, who offered use of the museum's board room for informal weekend presentations and discussions of the work of several young New York architects. The five architects who presented were distilled from a larger group that had been gathering since 1964 at the CASE meetings (Conference of Architects for the Study of the Environment) to discuss architectural theory and design, among them Robert Venturi, Vincent Scully, Eisenman, Graves, and Rowe, a group that Eisenman describes as the architectural "establishment of the East."[1] By the time of the MoMA presentations in 1969, Meier, Gwathmey, and Hejduk were part of a smaller group of five architects, with invited critics such as Rowe, Frampton, Anthony Vidler, and Stanford Anderson offering critiques. Each architect would present a single project that was then discussed and debated.

The MoMA gatherings begat the idea of documenting the presentations by collecting the projects and discussions in a pamphlet or (as the idea became more ambitious) between the covers of a book, to circulate the work and ideas to a wider audience. Eisenman, with the notion of publishing a book, approached George Wittenborn, the art book publisher.

The publication process was slow, Richard Meier remembers. At first each architect was allotted space for one project, and suitably publishable materials were collected. Then it was decided that a second project should be added, and more documentation was in order.[2] Color or not? It had been agreed that the book would be black and white, to keep costs down, but Hejduk wanted to present one project in color (his "House 10" became the only project to have a color page in the finished book). And what to call it? *Cardboard Architecture* was an early title suggested by Eisenman but rejected by the group; in fact a book title could never be agreed upon. When finally published in 1972 by Wittenborn & Company, it was, by default, *Five Architects: Eisenman, Graves, Gwathmey, Hejduk, Meier.*

Five Architects was republished in 1975 by Oxford University Press, with the addition of a postscript by Philip Johnson. Arthur Drexler wrote the foreword, in which he made clear his relief that these five architects "picked up where the thirties left off," and were engaged in "an architecture of rational poetry" rather than social engineering through built form. Colin Rowe's introduction was a deconstruction of the mythologies of the Modern movement. Modernism in America had been divested of its revolutionary agenda, observed Rowe, making it safe for capitalism. But even in socialist Europe, Modern architecture had failed to deliver the expected revolution. Its practice, believed Rowe, was disconnected from its theory. Given the theoretical bankruptcy of Modernism and its practical limitations, Rowe's position was that contemporary architects might explore other facets of the movement, such as its plastic and spatial inventions—in other words, its formalism. This is the program that the Five had pursued and presented in the book. Rowe speculated that in taking this tack, the Five raised legitimate questions about Modernism's unexamined assumptions regarding originality, creativity, precedent, authenticity, and the free will of the architect.[3]

In his critical essay, "Frontality vs. Rotation," Kenneth Frampton coolly dissected the work of the Five in a search for what holds these architects together as a group. Frampton's is a formal descriptive analysis: they're all Corbusian in exterior appearance; Eisenman is into layering; Graves and Meier are into frontality and rotation; Hejduk is freed from the dictates of client, program, or location. Gwathmey is the odd man out: his projects address buildability; the others are indifferent to building culture. For this reason, Frampton pronounced Gwathmey's work as the most American.[4] Johnson closes the collection with a brief postscript, wondering why these architects are all in the same book. He can't understand Eisenman, but he likes the pictures; Graves does great architecture as lawn furniture; Gwathmey is a fashion-conscious builder; Hejduk's drawings are magical; Meier learns from history.[5]

The stir started by *Five Architects* was at first contained mostly in the architectural salons of New York and along the academic axis running from Harvard through Yale to Princeton and Penn. It broke open when a second group, just as loosely connected as the Five, picked a fight with them, a skirmish that was published in the pages of *Architectural Forum* in May 1973. This group, known as the "Grays" in contrast to the Five "Whites," was assembled by Robert A.M. Stern, who saw an opportunity to spark an architectural dialogue about high design ideas that, he reflects, was sorely missing at the time.

"Peter Eisenman and I had shared similar feelings about architecture in the 1960s and the early '70s," says Stern. "We saw a stagnation of late Modernism. There were naïve, 'back to the woods' movements in architecture," such as what Dave Sellers was doing at Prickly Mountain, Vermont. "There was design based on populism, taking social surveys on the street, and basing design on what you learned by asking questions. I felt that this had trivialized architecture and its discourse. It wasn't design." Stern adds that he and Eisenman "… sort of invented each other, as foils. We saw what was happening as a collapse of standards, a collapse of artistic concerns. There was too much emphasis on the social agenda and 'popism.'"[6]

According to Stern, Eisenman suggested that he write a review of *Five Architects*. Then the two concocted an even better idea: a sort of architectural professional wrestling match, which became the landmark *Forum* article "Five on Five." The scenario was that five architects from the opposite ideological side of the fence would challenge the work and ideas presented in *Five Architects*. In contrast to the formal "purity" of the Whites, as the Five Architects were described (given their architectural heritage from Le Corbusier), Stern and his team would write from the viewpoint of the Grays, an inclusivist perspective that drew upon architecture's classical formal language and also found aesthetic delight in such ordinary places as the commercial strip and vulgar Vegas. Robert Venturi was the intellectual father of the Grays, but he declined to be enlisted by Stern in this skirmish. Stern drafted architects Jaquelin Robertson and Charles Moore for a critical siege on the Whites, then rounded out the quintet with architects Allan Greenberg and Romaldo Giurgola. Stern insisted that the five articles be tough and critical, qualities practically unheard of at a time when architects never publicly said nasty things about each other's work, let alone in print. When *Progressive Architecture* magazine turned the idea down, architectural journalist Suzanne Stephens, then an editor at *Forum*, approached her editor, William Marlin, with the idea. Stephens shepherded the articles through the editing process, making sure they pulled no punches. In a breach of journalistic protocol, according to Stephens, *Forum* agreed with Stern and Eisenman that the five critiques would be shown to the Five before the magazine went to press. *Forum* agreed since it was so unusual that architects would be taking their gloves off and criticizing other architects. The Five were not pleased.

"The Whites were starting their practices, teaching at Princeton," explains Stephens, "and they didn't want to be controversial. Graves said I was destroying his career. I said, 'On the contrary, you guys will be the ones that everyone wants on the lecture circuit.'" Stephens recalls that, shortly before publication of "Five on Five," Philip Johnson hosted a party for young architects at his 52nd Street townhouse. Eisenman approached Stephens about the tough tone of the articles. "Eisenman came up to me near the pool, saying, 'Hey, I'm told you made all those changes ... You're a troublemaker,' and I said, 'Peter, that means I'm writing five different kinds of critiques in five different styles. That makes me a genius. Keep it up, you're helping my critical career.' Then he stopped." As it happened, "Five on Five" was a sellout. "You couldn't find a copy," remembers Stephens. "And it was like all of these football teams started, and you were rooting for different teams. And all these years later, Stern and Eisenman are still working hand in hand."[7]

In late 1973, *Five Architects* and the debate about their work gained wider public attention. Eisenman remembers sitting at the breakfast table with his kids on a November morning, reading the

sports section of the *New York Times*, when his son remarked that daddy's picture was in the paper. Section 2 carried Paul Goldberger's article "Architecture's '5' Make Their Ideas Felt," which profiled the architects, their work, and what Goldberger saw as their particular stance: "...the talk of the New York architectural world today centers largely around a group of five architects who have rejected the notion of architecture as a social tool, rejected prefabrication, rejected the fads of computer design, mega-structures and other bits of super technology, and, instead have concentrated their efforts on what is perhaps the most traditional— and elevated—architectural problem of all: the making of form."[8]

In the radical architecture environment of the 1960s—designing for the counter-culture, engaging architecture's disenfranchised (minorities and the poor), and questioning authority—wanting just to make form was pretty radical, and was simultaneously deeply conservative for those in a profession that appeared to want to be socially relevant. This was at a time when the architectural profession was publically challenged for being completely out of touch with what was happening in society. In 1968, Whitney M. Young, Jr., head of the National Urban League, castigated the architectural profession at the national AIA Convention in Portland for turning a blind eye to racism: "...you are not a profession that has distinguished itself by your social and civic contributions to the cause of civil rights, and I am sure this has not come to you as any shock. You are most distinguished by your thunderous silence and your complete irrelevance."[9] The very year *Five Architects* appeared, the AIA gave architect Robert J. Nash the first Whitney M. Young, Jr., Award, which recognizes the social contributions to architecture by an architect or organization.

Goldberger characterizes the context of architectural discourse at that time as fairly boring. "This was not a particularly interesting time in architecture," he recalls. "The economy was stalled, not much was happening. There were no great faces on the horizon, no new practitioners. It was a flat landscape architecturally. Architectural culture was at an ebb, and *Five Architects* helped it to flow again."[10]

"*Five Architects* struck me as a New York moment," says Goldberger. Instead of dwelling on how architecture might function socially, the New York Five as Goldberger dubbed them, wanted to celebrate abstraction and form, the very meaning of the thing itself, as a work of architecture. "The New York Five were going against the grain," says Goldberger. "There were fresh architectural thoughts, ideas. The seeds of Postmodernism had begun to germinate, but this group of younger architects was saying that they weren't buying it." Goldberger maintains that the two camps, the Whites and the Grays, were really not that different, in terms of their beliefs about the role of architecture and the role of architects. "But there was something exciting about the dialogue. This had not been happening before."[11]

Michael Graves concurs that the publication of *Five Architects* seemed to mark a sea change in how architecture was talked about—both in schools and in public. The professional architectural journals were focused on finished buildings, the work of established older architects, what was being built in different cities around the country, and new building technology, but there was very little discussion about theoretical ideas in architecture. No opposing viewpoints were being presented in the journals. This lack of a vibrant theoretical culture pervaded even the schools, where architects who built were the primary focus of instruction. Few of the profession's celebrated architects were also teaching. *Five Architects*, notes Graves, seemed to open a floodgate of architectural ideas.

"With the Whites and the Grays, we wanted there to be a scene," says Graves, even if it was an orchestrated one. The result was the start of a lively lecture circuit. "Before this time," Graves recalls, "lectures were sedate, not controversial. There were no public pronouncements on architecture. At a lecture you had to submit your questions ahead of time for the lecturer to address."[12] Schools started to invite controversial figures, and swapped critics to provide opposing viewpoints. A critical architectural culture, which had long been a hallmark of the discipline in Europe, started to emerge in the U.S.

In the publishing world, *Five Architects* also marked the beginning of books and journals devoted to the work of a single architect or group of architects who weren't necessarily established practitioners. "*Five Architects* really started a market for the architectural monograph," notes Stern, waving his hand at a wall full of such books in his office at Yale, where I interviewed him about the book and its impact. Now there is a market for large-format architecture books (such as the one you are reading). As monographs grew in popularity, and younger architects who had not built very much were celebrated, there was less need for underground discourse, Stern says. Such publications became career builders—a form of instant architectural fame—instead of retrospectives of a vast body of work accomplished over years.

The need for underground architectural discourse persists, of course, among young architects without access to the archi-tectural publishing establishment. Although it's now easier to disseminate work than it has ever been, young architects gravitate toward discussing their work through such sites as blogspot, at face-to-face get-togethers such as Pecha Kucha (present your work and ideas in 20 slides, each for 20 seconds), and at lectures such as those held at the Storefront for Art and Architecture in New York.

For Goldberger, the publication of *Five Architects* can be seen as the start of the golden age of the celebrity architect (the same moment when others in creative niches—celebrity chefs and celebrity dress designers—caught the public's attention). "Architectural publicity was not as pervasive then as it is now," says Goldberger. High-fashion architecture and star architects have become consumer products for those not necessarily in the market to hire an architect. There were traces of this development before *Five Architects*, of course, particularly in the careers of such vigorous self-promoters as Frank Lloyd Wright and Le Corbusier. But *Five Architects,* with a white cover with just the architects' names in black without images of their work (an homage to the Beatles' *White Album*), signaled the arrival of the architectural celebrity.

How are the members of the New York Dozen like, and not like, the New York Five? Unlike the Five, the Dozen did not volunteer to be included in a book; they were selected from a variety of sources. A number were winners in MoMA's Young Architects program, which each year since 1999 selects a young firm to design a project for MoMA's PS1 in Long Island City. Others had been published in *Oculus*, the journal of the AIA New York Chapter, which regularly identifies emerging talent. Observers of New York's architectural landscape also provided leads.

An early hope for this book was that the survivors of the original Five might have a hand in selecting the Dozen; alas, Hejduk died in 2000 and Gwathmey succumbed to cancer while this book was being prepared. Eisenman, Graves, and Meier were less interested in anointing a new generation than they continue to be in their own work which, I suppose, is the hallmark of all architectural over-achievers.

As a group, the Dozen have about as much cohesion as the original Five. They can't be seen as a "New York School," as some attempted, with little success, to portray the Five. They have a strong sense of the role New York plays in their practice—something that *Five Architects* never addressed. For the Dozen, the city functions as an incubator, a battery, a prompt, a laboratory, a stimulant, a distraction, an exhilaration, an escape, an endless dichotomy. Or, as one of the Dozen puts it: New York is important for its physical, intellectual, and cultural density.

As a group, the members of the Dozen are more interested than the Five ever were in the collaborative nature of architectural design, fabrication, and practice. This seems to be a generational trait and a product of the "social media" milieu in which these architects operate. Many of the firms identify themselves less as corporate entities (with a roster of names on the door) than as workshops, clusters, and platforms for collaboration with other architects, fabricators, software designers, and material scientists. Compared with the Five, the Dozen approach architecture far less as an abstraction, much more hands-on, and as an opportunity to work with others on a problem. Architectural historian Gwendolyn Wright has used the word "constellation" to describe the web of relationships among "stars" (architectural and otherwise), allowing us to see them and their work in a larger, more complex context.[13] Architect and historian Beverly Willis expands on Wright's analogy in characterizing young architects as particularly more prone to working in constellations of practice: groups of architects, who through technology and temperament, align with other professionals to create ensembles that play together and collaborate on a single project, then disperse. (Willis further suggests that the model of the movie industry's academy awards might be adopted by the architectural profession to more accurately recognize the constellations of talent necessary to achieve the complex, broadly based architectural projects of today.)[14]

If you peruse the register of collaborators listed by each of the dozen firms profiled in this book, you find many of the same names, corroborating the constellation structure advocated by Wright and Willis. Many of the firms in this book mention collaborators within the office, as well as outside the practice. "The art of architecture," as one of the Dozen describes it, "has a collaborative heart."

The New York Five were consistent in their pursuit of architecture as a fine art, which they viewed as the highest form of achievement—a reinstatement of the architect's historical role. While aesthetics and form making are important to the Dozen, they are less willing, in describing their work, to draw a tight, formalistic circle around the discipline of architecture itself. In fact, cross-disciplinary interests—in ecology, art, material science, digital media, urban design, construction, human perception and psychology, economics, sustainability—appear often in their work. Ironically, the 1970s was a high-water mark of interest in interdisciplinary approaches to architecture; one that the Five, you

could argue, reacted against. "Lines between disciplines do not exist," declares one of the Dozen. Socially conscious design, especially within the context of sustainability, and architecture with a civic/public role, are prominent in the work of many of the Dozen.

Demographically and geographically, the Dozen are more diverse and expansive than the Five of 40 years ago. This is certainly not a boys-only club. Women principals populate about half the firms, and many of the firm founders are ethnically and culturally diverse. Many of the Dozen pursue or have built projects on other continents, a reflection of the global stage that architecture is practiced on today.

The Dozen's affinity for collaboration, cross-disciplinary pursuits, social media connections, and diversity within the mix all point to an edginess with the star architect system as we know it. Evidence of this erupted while this book was being prepared: *New York Times* architecture critic Nicolai Ouroussoff published an article about the passing of Charles Gwathmey, in which he wrote wistfully about the days of the New York Five and the dearth of architectural heroes today in the Big Apple. After the heyday of the New York Five, Ouroussoff observed, architectural energy and innovation shifted to Los Angeles, and New York has yet to recapture the architectural intensity it once had.

Ouroussoff's article triggered a rebuke from Andrew Bernheimer whose firm, Della Valle Bernheimer, is profiled in this book. Contrary to the critic's lament, Bernheimer wrote in "An Open Letter to Nicolai Ouroussoff" in the online magazine *Design Observer,* there are dozens of influential architects practicing in New York and building around the globe.[15] And, just as important, many are teaching at and heading celebrated schools of architecture (several of the architects in the New York Dozen teach or have taught at Yale, Harvard, Princeton, Columbia, Parsons, and other programs, and are regulars on the national architecture school lecture circuit).

Were Ouroussoff to buy a MetroCard, as Bernheimer proposed, and visit the architectural studios "… that are energetically creating new work in our diverse city," the *Times* critic would find countless other studios and offices "… run by architects, young (and in some cases significantly younger than the accomplished Angelenos he mentions) men and women, all of whom have had broad influence within and outside the profession. Most of these practices and the people who run them, including our own, have devoted themselves to a dual act of responsibly progressive design: teaching and building. They have already had (even though considered mere youngsters in a profession that rewards age and patience) an impact on local and more far-flung colleagues and students, on this generation and future generations of architects, and on New York City itself."[16]

The responses to Bernheimer's open letter were pro and con, but the most cogent made a distinction between an earlier generation of self-promotional architects and the young New York architects who practice today in what they described as thoughtful and responsible ways. "I think attention to the stars in our system detracts from the more important and consistent architecture produced by the many, often struggling firms that make up the backbone of the design community," wrote one respondent. Another called Ouroussoff's attention to the damage done to New York by such heroic stars of the past, "much of which did harm to the cityscape." Yet another faulted the *New York Times* critic for his focus on object-oriented architecture in a city where the best design is often fabric oriented.

Many of the projects in this book are integrated into the existing fabric in New York and other cities, and bear out the qualitative challenge of designing fabric over object. The past 40 years since *Five Architects*, fixated as the book and most of this period were on architectural objects, point to the environmental and urban injury wrought by such a myopic design perspective. New work by young architects can just as easily be faulted for object worship, as can any of the twisted and rotated fancies of Eisenman and company. But today, thankfully, architectural insertions in urban fabrics are judged by much tougher standards than they were during the days of the New York Five. The environmental impact of such designs is more carefully assessed, and the new generation of architects takes architecture's carbon footprint into their design deliberations. They are more attuned not only to architecture's ecological impact, but also to the role of nature as a design generator and the fusion of architecture and landscape in landform design.

One might argue that because it was a different time and place, with different value systems, we cannot fault the New York Five and their generation for not caring about the environmental impact of their buildings, the damage their architecture might cause to cities, or the social cost of their creations. The New York Five asserted that beyond mere problem solving, architectural design had a larger responsibility to art, to ideas, to critical theory, to discourse. But today's New York Dozen, and dozens more like them, need also to be aware that architectural values such as socially responsible design, environmental sustainability, and attention to the larger fabric of place-making were part of the discourse in the 1960s and 70s. For example, a straight line can be drawn from the

architectural profession's role in energy conservation 40 years ago to today's sustainable architecture. Neighborhood preservation, evidence-based design, and the science of liveable cities all have theoretical roots in the 1960s or earlier. These were a few of the other currents in the 1960s and 70s—along with the staid creations of the corporate architectural establishment—that the New York Five reacted against.

Of course, today's Dozen and its generation have their own blind spots, such as the fetish of seductive computer rendering, and a formal fascination for architectural blobs that raise the question of human habitation. They are not shy about promoting their own work, as their willingness to be part of *New York Dozen* demonstrates. But their commitment to socially relevant design and to architectural experimentation that leads to buildable solutions, in addition to advancing architecture as an art, seems genuine and sound.

It appears that you *can* learn something from the example of your elders.

NOTES

1 Interview with Peter Eisenman, New York, NY, March 18, 2009.
2 Interview with Richard Meier, New York, NY, March 18, 2009.
3 Colin Rowe, "Introduction," in *Five Architects*, New York: Oxford University Press, 1975, p. 7.
4 Kenneth Frampton, "Frontality vs. Rotation," in *Five Architects*, New York: Oxford University Press, 1975, pp. 9–13.
5 Philip Johnson, "Postscript," in *Five Architects*, New York: Oxford University Press, 1975, p. 138.
6 Interview with Robert A.M. Stern, New Haven, CT, December 3, 2009.
7 Telephone interview with Suzanne Stephens, December 12, 2009.
8 Paul Goldberger, "Architecture's '5' Make Their Ideas Felt," *The New York Times*, November 26, 1973, pp. 33, 52.
9 "Unedited transcript of the speech made to the American Institute of Architects in 1968," in *20 on 20/20 Vision: Perspectives on Diversity and Design*, edited by Linda Kiisk, Boston Society of Architects, http://www.architects.org/emplibrary/20_on_2020_Vision.pdf, p. 16, accessed January 2, 2011.
10 Interview with Paul Goldberger, New York, NY, June 10, 2009.
11 Ibid.
12 Interview with Michael Graves, Princeton, NJ, March 19, 2009.
13 Gwendolyn Wright, "Women in Modernism," paper presented at the colloquium, *Women and Modernism: Making Places in Architecture*, The Beverly Willis Architecture Foundation with the Museum of Modern Art, October 25, 2007.
14 Beverly Willis, "Fabricating Identity," University of Hartford Department of Architecture Lecture Series, April 22, 2009.
15 Andrew Bernheimer, "An Open Letter to Nicolai Ouroussoff," *Design Observer*, http://observatory.designobserver.com/entry.html?entry=10537, accessed January 2, 2011.
16 Ibid.

Andre Kikoski Architect

180 Varick Street, Suite 1316, New York, New York, 10014

www.akarch.com

WE DESIGN DRAMATIC, INVENTIVE, TEXTURAL SPACES.

WHO WE ARE:
Andre Kikoski, AIA LEED AP

OUR ARCHITECTURAL VALUES IN A DOZEN WORDS:
We strive for deft clarity and technical precision to create contemporary artistry.

OUR ARCHITECTURAL PHILOSOPHY IN THREE-DOZEN WORDS:
We create projects that are innovative, tactile, and striking. While it is important that the image of a project is compelling, it is also just as important that the closer you look, the better it gets.

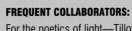

FREQUENT COLLABORATORS:

For the poetics of light—Tillotson Design Associates
For the unimagined material capabilities—Peterson Geller Spurge and Amuneal
For beautiful photography—Peter Aaron at Esto
For inspiration, both bold and intimate—Manhattan itself

OUR PRACTICE IN TWENTY-DOZEN WORDS:

Andre Kikoski Architect is a Manhattan-based, multi-disciplinary design firm committed to artistic innovation regardless of budget, genre, or client. Our passions for material research and details, as well as our client-centric approach, have won the firm many prestigious projects in a wide range of categories—from hospitality to arts and culture, and real estate to high-end residential.

Our design process starts by investigating the essential ideas surrounding each new commission. We mine visual references, precedents, and cultural associations for their relevance. These inspirations help us to answer the particular questions of each project, and produce a singular, inevitable design solution. Ultimately, ours is an architecture of strong ideas.

We practice collaboratively, both within the office and with our team of consultants, fabricators, and manufacturers. This approach produces aesthetic innovations and technical solutions that push the limits of contemporary design and that create elegant, well-resolved works of the highest technical criteria.

A special focus of the office is creating engaging new buildings in transitional neighborhoods and transforming landmark buildings such as our recently completed projects within the Guggenheim Museum. The office has four contemporary projects along New York's established Museum Mile on Fifth Avenue, including the interiors of the residential tower over the Museum for African Art.

Among the firm's laurels is an Award of Excellence from the AIA/NY; a James Beard Foundation Award for Outstanding Restaurant Design; two Lumen Awards for Lighting Excellence; and the Edwin Guth Memorial Award for lighting.

WHY WE PRACTICE IN NEW YORK IN TWO-DOZEN WORDS:

Because New York is a still a place where anything is possible and the stimulating social experience constantly introduces exciting new people and ideas.

Eaglebrook School Art Center
Deerfield, Massachusetts

The design for the Eaglebrook School Art Center disperses studios and performance spaces within three pavilions and an internalized campus pathway, creating communal spaces for gathering, performances, and exhibition.

The pavilion volumes become visually complex as they rotate in plan and their rooflines angle away from each other. Clad in a layer of vertical wooden fins and structural glass walls, the diaphanous skin of the 10,000-square-foot building dissolves elegantly into the surrounding forest.

The Art Center engages perspective, motion, and materiality to create a thoughtful harmony between the activity of the studios and the school's setting. It offers a new identity for the arts at Eaglebrook School.

1 Entry
2 Wood shop
3 Restroom
4 Closet
5 Elevator
6 Theater
7 Back of house mechanical
8 Practice room
9 Ceramics

0   12ft

1

2

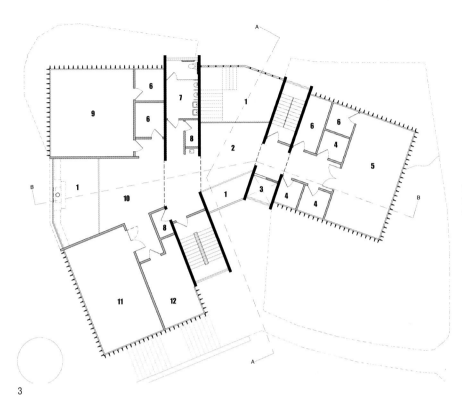

3

1 Open to below
2 Sculpture bridge
3 Elevator
4 Practice room
5 Stone
6 Faculty office
7 Restroom
8 Closet
9 Chorus
10 Student lounge gallery
11 Painting
12 Stained glass

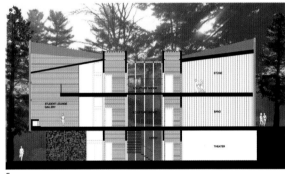

5

1 First floor plan 2 Interior rendering at sculpture bridge and
lounge 3 Third floor plan 4 Second floor plan 5 Rendered
building section

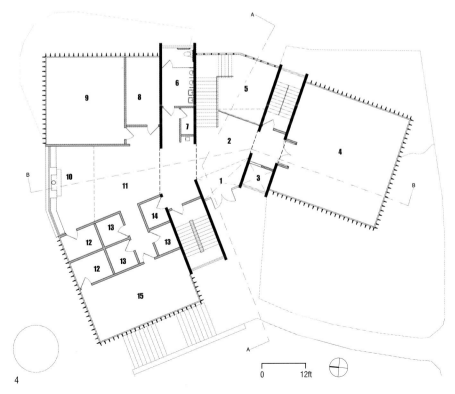

4

1 Double-height entry
2 Sculpture bridge
3 Elevator
4 Band
5 Open to entry
6 Restroom
7 Closet
8 Publishing
9 Photography
10 Hearth
11 Student lounge gallery
12 Faculty office
13 Practice room
14 Storage
15 Architecture

0   12ft

Café 3 at the Guggenheim Museum
New York, New York

1 Café 3 looking through the Monitor atrium **2** View of console showing Central Park Reservoir beyond **3** Detail of torqued seamless console **4** Café 3 looking through the Monitor atrium **following pages** Looking back to Café 3 bar and cantilevered console
Peter Aaron/Esto; AKA; Eric Laignel

The shapes of Frank Lloyd Wright's iconic building are nuanced to create inventive forms for an elliptical espresso bar and attenuated tapered counters, echoing the building's plasticity. They abstract the spatial sequence of spiraling through the rotunda, bringing energy and movement to 850 square feet off the Kandinsky Gallery overlooking Central Park.

Constructed entirely of seamless white Corian, these pure elements are calm and inviting; they respond distinctly to subtle variations in light. Though complex in geometry, their discreet calligraphy disappears. With modesty and restraint, they enliven this first addition to the interior of Wright's celebrated work with a precise vision of movement, form, and surprise.

1

2

3

4

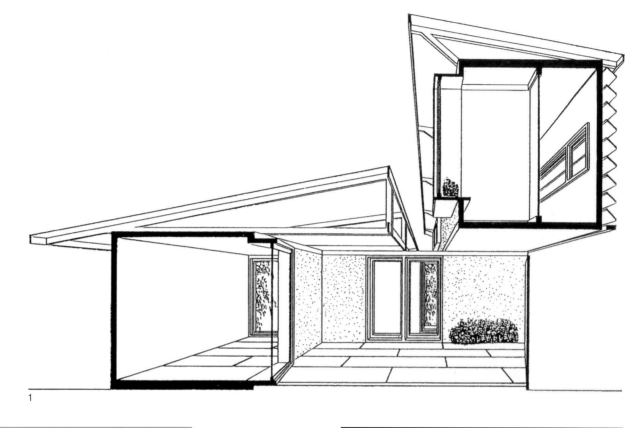

1

The Container House prototype was commissioned by Genstar Container Corporation. Target markets are high-density, urban port locations in Asia, Africa, and Latin America where surplus containers and the infrastructure to deal with them are already in place. The 660-square-foot, two-level unit contains a living room, kitchen, full bath, two bedrooms, and a spare room. Dual courtyards are sheltered to expand living, cooking, and workspace over a compact 40-foot-by-28-foot lot. The open layout of the building section provides cross-ventilation and thermal convection to make the house comfortable year-round.

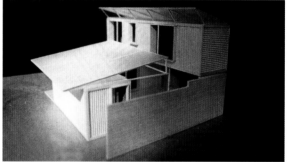

2

1 Perspective drawing showing view to internal courtyard **2** Photo of model showing roof overhangs (for cooling and ventilation) [top]; showing view to internal courtyard [bottom] **3** Exploded axonometric view showing kit of parts that will be attached to containers **4** Second floor plan **5** First floor plan **AKA**

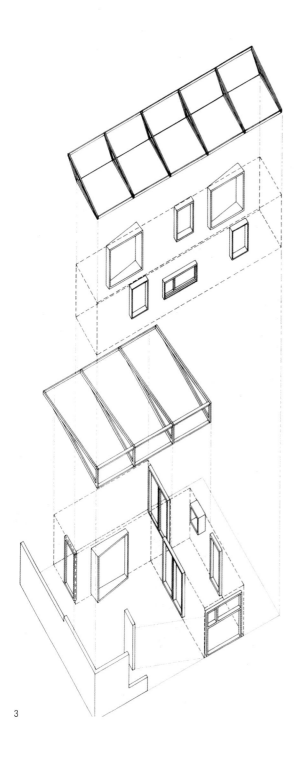

3

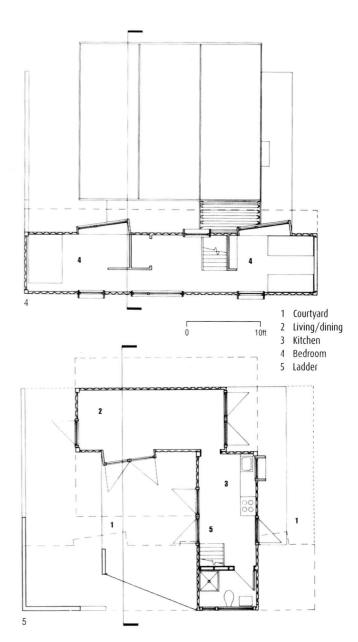

4

1 Courtyard
2 Living/dining
3 Kitchen
4 Bedroom
5 Ladder

0   10ft

5

Second Home Kitchen and Bar
Denver, Colorado

The design transforms what was once a single 5,000-square-foot venue into a series of intimate spaces that feel like a mountain retreat. The sober geometry of the plan is complemented by unembellished dry-stack stone walls and rough-hewn wood plank ceilings. Dramatic lighting showcases the organic textures of the Rocky Mountains. Bold design elements within these bounds—such as laminated glass fins made from salvaged wood, 1950s Italian chandeliers, graffiti-covered Danish chairs, turn-of-the-19th-century Viennese Secessionist banquettes, hide-upholstered walls, and shearling furniture—keep things light hearted. Inventive, dramatic, and highly tactile, the design is a pure expression of the designer's sensibility.

1

2

3

1 Dining room showing detail of local stone piers and wood plank ceiling **2** Detail of salvaged wood glass fins **3** Overall view of bar and lounge **Eric Laignel**

4 Courtyard showing linear gas fire element and fabric brise-soleil **5** Detail of live bark wall in private dining room **6** Overall view of dining room and wine cellar **7** Bar detail **Eric Laignel**

4

5

6

Wright Restaurant, Guggenheim Museum

New York, New York

1 View into the restaurant from the entry **2** View of the interior from rear of the space **3** Overall view from rear of space **4** Detail view of ceiling canopy and communal table **5** Detail view of custom chair **6** Overall view of dining room
Peter Aaron/Esto

The design of the Wright Restaurant at the Guggenheim Museum references and transforms the building's architecture and geometries. Playful forms and dynamic movement through this 1,600-square-foot space imbue it with novelty and intrigue. The materials and colors include a curvilinear wall of walnut layered with illuminated fiber-optics; a bar clad in a shimmering skin of innovative custom metalwork and topped in seamless white Corian; a sweeping banquette with vivid blue leather seating backed by illuminated planes of woven gray texture; and a layered ceiling canopy of taut white membrane. Together these materials and colors form a perfect complement to the site-specific collaborative artwork with artist Liam Gillick that has been commissioned for the space.

1

2

3

4

5

6

The Yankee Club
Yankee Stadium, Bronx, New York

Fully designed, executed, and opened in 12 weeks, this 4,000-square-foot restaurant at Yankee Stadium is a contemporary interpretation of the heroes and icons that made the team. The design abstracts signature elements such as the iconic stadium frieze and draws from the physics of the sport itself. The trajectory of a curve-ball pitch organizes the movement of patrons through the space. Ash and oak wood, glove leather, and baseballs become millwork and paneling: there is a bar upholstered with glove leather, a sculptural banquette, and an entry rotunda emblazoned with the team's logo. Innovative design and fast-track delivery created a successful bond between the space and the sport in record time.

1

2

3

4

5

1 Detail view of entry rotunda
2 Detail view of dining room
3 Overall view of restaurant
interior 4 Detail view of
signature Yankee frieze
5 Detail view of bar
David Sundberg/Esto

Architecture in Formation PC

526 West 26th Street, Suite 422, New York, New York, 10001

www.aifny.com

EXPLOITING APPROPRIATE TECHNOLOGIES, SERVICING ENVIRONMENTAL CIRCUMSTANCE.

OUR ARCHITECTURAL VALUES IN A DOZEN WORDS:
prudent / audacious
logical / sensual
analytical / intuitive
specific / universal
spatial / tactile
analog / digital

WHO WE ARE:
A small team of four to six architects and designers led by Matthew Bremer, AIA, Principal.

OUR ARCHITECTURAL PHILOSOPHY IN THREE-DOZEN WORDS:
Architecture is the product of a slow alchemy comprised of bricks, mortar, smoke, mirrors, pixels, pencils, solitude, discourse, and a richly lived life, practiced with prudence and audacity: a constantly watchful eye and inordinate blind faith.

OUR PRACTICE IN TWENTY-DOZEN WORDS:

Our practice revels in an impassioned pursuit of creating inspired spaces, places, objects, and landscapes within the disciplines of architecture and design. The name Architecture in Formation is intended to suggest our belief in the collaborative act of *making* within the larger professional process. While strong conceptual convictions undergird each project, the work is not overly theoretical. We take on a wide range of project types at a variety of scales. Each project is approached with a consistent level of rigorous and sensitive investigation, with a design process and project delivery method tailored to the unique parameters of the job. Understanding the appropriate relationships between a work and its expanded physical and cultural context allows for the development of an inventive yet appropriate detail language that stems from these unique conditions. This is why there is no overarching digital or manual, formal or technical obsession in the work as a whole, and rarely do our projects look alike. Essential to the work is the shared belief that design integrity is rooted in a spirited process of analysis, intuition, development, refinement, and implementation.

Our practice is really not unlike architecture itself: it is organic, it must breathe and be able to expand and contract, adapting its purpose in order to sustain itself and remain useful. Perhaps the one consistent thread running through all our projects is the desire to achieve an end result for users that is both obvious and unexpected.

WHY WE PRACTICE IN NEW YORK IN TWO-DOZEN WORDS:

O.M.G.
Another R.S.V.P.
A.D.D.
O.C.D.
N.Y.C.
U.O.N.
T.B.D....
Right?

FREQUENT COLLABORATORS:

Associated Fabrications (CNC milling, digital fabrication)
Bowery Restaurant Supply (custom stainless steel fabrication)
Curtis + Ginsberg Architects
Ross Dalland (structural engineering)
Espasso Inc. (fabrication and furnishings)
Ferra Inc. (metal work)
Filament33 Inc./Marianne Maloney (lighting design)
FXFowle Architects
Pocock: Design Environment (landscape)
Pro-Tone Contracting (residential interiors)
Rader + Crews (landscape)

PAST AND PRESENT DESIGN STAFF:

Fabian Bedolla
Dan Bracy
Koray Duman
Paulo Flores
Daniel Hui
Ricardo Kendall
Victor Ortega
Ricardo Vargas
John Zeien
Tom Zook

1

House for a butcher and an art maven
Long Island, New York

This house strikes a delicate balance between modesty and majesty within the surrounding landscape. The site is a heavily wooded 3-acre property on the North Shore of Long Island with an existing house that the clients have occupied since they wed more than 30 years ago. The couple wanted to re-conceive their newly empty nest to better suit their active, social lifestyle. The existing house consisted of two wings—a long, low-slung 1970s "ranch-burger deluxe" in front, and a large master suite added in the late 1980s by Andrew Geller, Raymond Lowey's partner, well-known for his small wooden mid-century beach bungalows in the Hamptons and on Fire Island.

The solution was ostensibly a teardown of the original suburban tract house and a major re-conception of the entire grounds. It marries new to existing by three simple yet precise moves—a cut, a fold, and a stitch. The private portion of the existing front house is partially maintained, while an entirely new public wing framed in steel and clad in glass, cypress, and mahogany is sutured back in to it. By slicing along two diagonals of the existing pitched roof, two "winglets" were folded up from the previous line

of the house. This move more than doubled the light and views flooding into the main living spaces. Further, the new wing is "stitched" back seamlessly to the existing house. The detached four-car garage casually shows off the owners' car collection in much the same manner that the house quietly integrates a significant collection of artwork by emerging and established contemporary artists.

The beauty, drama, and efficiency of the site's natural features become the source of inspiration for the project. Views out and winter sun in have been maximized via vast double-glazed low-E windows, cross ventilation has been exploited, and rainwater reused to create an enviably efficient house.

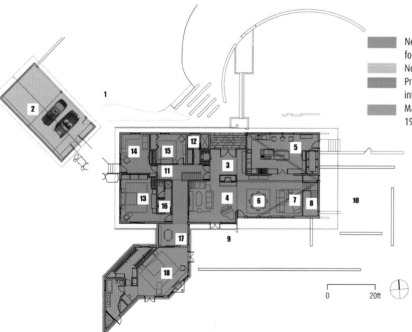

2

3

New public wing extension to original house on
footprint of demolished original public zone

New detached four-car garage

Private wing of original tract house, renovated
into guest wing, 2005-2006

Master suit wing addition by Andrew Geller,
1986, renovated 2005-2006

1	Park court	10	East courtyard
2	New detached four-car garage	11	Guest wing hall
3	Foyer	12	Powder room/guest bath
4	Media room	13	Guest room
5	Kitchen	14	Guest room/his study
6	Dining area	15	Guest room
7	Sitting area	16	Guest bath
8	Stair to her office below	17	Gallery/library
9	Rear (south) terrace	18	Master suite

0   20ft

1 Front view of house during autumn **2** View of east façade from
sunken side courtyard **3** Entrance: east view from garden wall
gate **4** Ground floor plan **Tom Powell**

4

5 View from her office/studio below through staircase to double-height living area above 6 Interior view of public living space along central spine 7 Interior view of sitting area 8 Night view of the interior **Tom Powell**

5

6

7

1

ESPASSO
New York, New York

A longstanding appreciation of Brazil's highly expressive modern-design legacy led to research into the sustainable millworking practices used there. A custom-fabrication collaboration between Architecture in Formation and the exclusive U.S. dealer representing the best of contemporary and vintage 20th-century Brazilian design developed into a commission to design a new TriBeCa flagship for Espasso, and subsequently, their LA showroom as well as the Espasso booth at Design Miami | Art Basel | Miami Beach in 2006.

The daring formal exploration of Oscar Neimeyer, the rarified artisan prowess of Joaquim Tenreiro's or Sergio Rodrigues' wood furniture, and Roberto Burle-Marx's painterly landscapes that seem visually synonymous with the city of Rio are certainly the best known examples of the relationship of form to place in Brazil. Despite the country's well-know difficulties controlling the rampant deforestation of its unmatchable yet irreplaceable natural resource—the Amazon rainforest—contemporary Brazilian design, now more than ever, is being sensitive to the materials from which it builds.

Providing a suitable yet compelling environment for the presentation of Brazilian design meant going beyond the predictably tasteful designer showroom, or the bland white-box gallery. Converting 8,000 square feet of the ground and cellar floors of a former garment factory in TriBeCa produced a subtly rich spatial and sensory experience that quietly references, yet dramatically frames, an ancestral history of contemporary Brazilian design. The TriBeCa showroom backdrops play on conventional figure–field relationships in unexpected ways, complementing and challenging the unique pieces without imitating them. The result is an environment where customers are educated through experience about Brazil and its design legacy, in a space that stands alone as a powerful piece of interior architecture.

1 Overall view of the ground floor looking across the stair towards the restroom cube **2** Display and seating platforms are extruded from the dramatic central ceremonial stair
Tom Powell

2

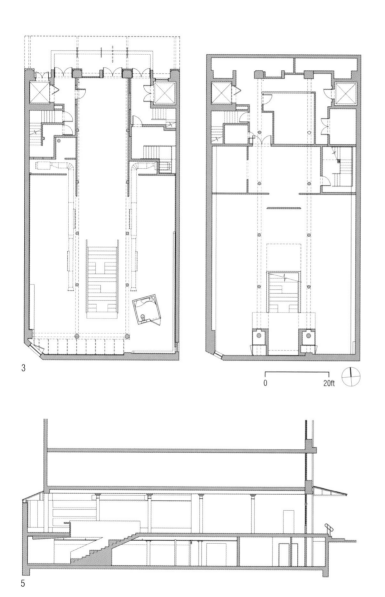

3

4

0   20ft

5

6

3 Floor plans **4** Public restroom volume: concealed **5** Section **6** Public restroom volume: exposed **7** At the cellar level light striates the masonry foundation wall of the six-story loft building it supports **8** Detail of the vanity inside public restroom box **9** View from the back across the main stair towards the entry gallery **Tom Powell**

7

8

9

Navy Green Master Plan
Brooklyn, New York

The map labels include:

- CLERMONT AVENUE (80'-0" R.O.W.)
- B.Q.E. (160'-0" R.O.W.)
- PARK AVENUE
- FLUSHING AVENUE (70'-0" R.O.W.)
- VANDERBILT AVENUE (80'-0" R.O.W.)
- R3 BUILDING / 8 FL 106'-4"
- 10 TOWNHOUSES / 4 FL
- R1 BUILDING / 12 FL 136'-11" / 11 FL 125'-11" / 8 FL 97'-11"
- COMMUNITY FACILITY/ COMMERCIAL / 2 FL 36'-10"
- EXISTING BUILDING
- SUPPORTIVE HOUSING / 8 FL 100'-11"
- 13 TOWNHOUSES / 4 FL / 8 FL 98'-7"
- R2 BUILDING / 12 FL 135'-7" / 11 FL 124'-7"
- 7 FL 97'-10" / 6 FL 87'-4" / 6 FL 87'-4"

The Navy Green Master Plan is the winning submission for the re-development of a 103,000-square-foot site occupying almost an entire city block in the Wallabout neighborhood of Brooklyn, previously occupied by the Brooklyn Navy Yard site. The New York City Department of Housing Preservation & Development sponsored the competition. The design team consisted of FX Fowle Architects, Curtis + Ginsberg Architects, Architecture in Formation, and Rader + Crews Landscape Architecture. The project was developed by Dunn Development Corp, L&M Development Partners, and the Pratt Area Community Council (PACC). The plan creates a unique, mixed-use community by combining affordable rental and home-owner units with market-rate co-ops, townhouses, and supportive housing facilities. Most unique to the project is the creation of a large courtyard shared by all residents, including supportive housing residents.

The PACC Navy Green Supportive Housing building is an eight-story, 60,000-square-foot, 98-unit residence for formerly homeless and low-income single adults, offering much-needed permanent, affordable housing in the community. The project is being developed and managed by PACC with on-site social services offered by Brooklyn Community Housing and Services. It is one of four in the master plan. Architecture in Formation is the design architect, and Curtis + Ginsberg Architects is the architect of record.

The project integrates single-occupancy studio apartments into an inviting community environment that strings together a range of shared communal spaces to engage residents in social inter-action that becomes a catalyst for fostering a sense of belonging. These spaces include a community room, a tenant meeting room that allows for vocational training, a shared outdoor courtyard space, and a large double-height space encapsulating entry, lobby, residents' lounge, and mail area. At the heart of this space is the Amphitheater, which offers casual areas for sitting and socializing along a path towards the courtyard.

2

1 Master plan: site plan (Courtesy FX Fowle Architects) **2** View of the lobby, Amphitheatre, and residents' lounge from the rear courtyard **3** Street view of PACC Navy Green Supportive Housing building **4** View of the Amphitheatre in the PACC Navy Green Supportive Housing building **5** View of PACC Navy Green Supportive Housing building as seen from the Brooklyn/Queens Expressway

Architecture in Formation PC

3

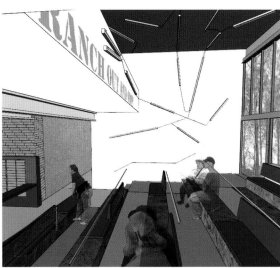

4

5

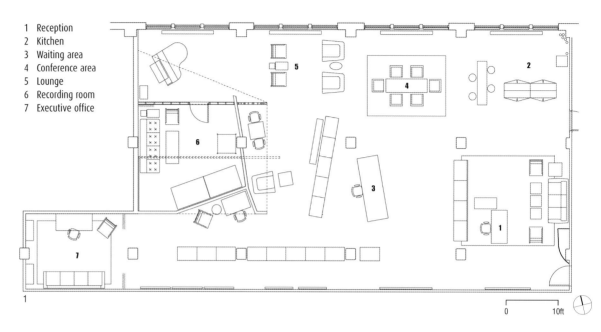

1 Floor plan 2 The "overhang" of the recording studio frames the piano 3&6 View west toward the recording studio 4 Recording studio 5 View along the north-facing window wall 7 Detail of the salon-style hanging of artworks in the executive office 8 Detail of the Plexiglas wall, which brings soft-filtered north light into the recording studio **Architecture in Formation PC**

1 Reception
2 Kitchen
3 Waiting area
4 Conference area
5 Lounge
6 Recording room
7 Executive office

1

0   10ft

Tonal Studio
New York, New York

This 3,000-square-foot West Chelsea commercial loft space is home to the executive offices and production studios for a creative resource company. New York-based Tonal has a strong Los Angeles presence and is known primarily for its sound scores for movies, television commercials, and environmental retail installations. Tonal sought a place to create original music and new ideas in a creative environment that would host clients and collaborators from advertising, network television, motion pictures, record labels, and design.

The build-out of the space, executed on a shoestring budget, was heavily influenced by the client's desire to showcase their collection of contemporary artwork by young emerging artists as well as French and American furniture from the 1940s through to the 1980s. The only "structural" requirement was a soundproof recording room. Otherwise, the space could be left open and raw. Most importantly, the client wanted to fuse their New York/LA lifestyles and sensibilities, sort of a "Hollywood Hills Case-Study-house-on-crack, in a Chelsea loft, on a dime."

2

3

4

5

6

7

8

Arts Corporation

Great Jones Street, New York, New York, 10012

artscorporation.com

ARCHITECTURE TECHNOLOGY
FURNITURE FILM
ART SCULPTURE

WHO WE ARE:
Mike Latham, director, and the Arts
Corporation

OUR ARCHITECTURAL VALUES IN A DOZEN WORDS:
Lines between disciplines do not exist.

Our work serves to investigate interstices.

OUR ARCHITECTURAL PHILOSOPHY IN THREE-DOZEN WORDS:
Materials and program, with the least possible intervention from
the individual, create the most rational architecture. The world is
difficult enough without gratuitous criteria. Architecture starts with
detail, and every detail is part of the architecture.

WHY WE PRACTICE IN NEW YORK IN TWO-DOZEN WORDS:

New York is a distracting juggernaut. When used to benefit, there's no substitute. Working on anything in New York in 2011 is being everywhere.

OUR PRACTICE IN 20-DOZEN WORDS:

In 2000 Mike Latham formed Arts Corporation, a multimedia design firm that integrated his varied interests in architecture, art, and technology. The firm serves as the backbone for Latham's work in architecture, furniture design, and product design, and a springboard for his innovative work in sculpture and film.

In response to the economic realities of a new practice, small-scale commissions were frequently accepted and built to fit within third-party architectural designs. Building from the details up, disciplines such as sculpture and furniture manufacture became increasingly integral to the firm's work. The inclusion of such work in several important collections of art, and its integration into its surroundings, were founding goals of the firm. Economical and speculative work such as the Arts Corporation's loft and workspace in Brooklyn resulted in additional commissions for art and architectural work at larger scales.

Balancing the diverse work of the Arts Corporation has been a constant focus. In 2003 Latham was granted the Young Architects Award by the Architectural League of New York, and in 2005 he was commissioned to design a functional sculpture for the premier issue of *Men's Vogue*. Current projects include the art film *Business Plan*, the story of the rise of Arts Corporation, and Arts Corporation's girl band, the Acettes.

Central themes in the firm's architecture, design, and art are an affinity for transparency, both physical and theoretical, movement over time, and incorporating the contemporary technology that surrounds us in unexpected ways.

FREQUENT COLLABORATORS:
Burch Borges
Jen Campbell
Magnus Bischofberger
Baier Bischofberger
Cora Sheibani
Jane Stubbs
Steven Learner Associates
Aaron Cattani
Cardinal Investments
Jan Krugier Gallery
Leo Koenig
karlssonwilker
The North Ferry
Disposable Television
Cinecycle
David Park
Crystal Campbell
Eric Goebel
Sneh Kadakia

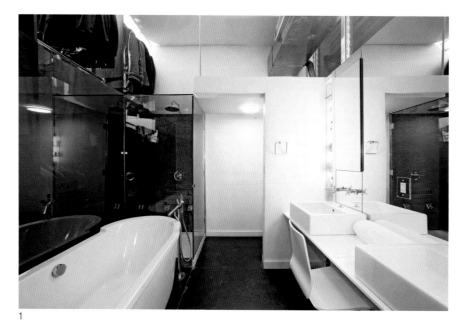

Arts Corporation Headquarters
New York, New York

1 Master bath **2** Mobile shower **3** Vitrines **4** Private loft **5** Dining room **6** Library (closed)

Evan Joseph; Hagen Stier

Arts Corporation Headquarters, located on Great Jones Street in Manhattan, serves as both a studio space where objects are crafted and the headquarters for day-to-day operations. The studio space is an all-encompassing artwork where the envelope and everything inside it are part of the work.

The studio features items such as the Arts Corporation vitrine, which can be fitted out as a kitchen, library, or closet, and in this case is primarily used to house sculptural supplies. A mobile bar in the kitchen area and a mobile shower demonstrate the frontiers of the corporation's research. At any given time, prototypes of various sculptures and inventions, such as the MP3 lounge, will be on display. The work desks are also custom Arts Corporation pieces.

Arts Corporation does business 24 hours a day with Zurich, Mexico City, and Tokyo, so it's not surprising that the principal, Mike Latham, has devised a way of living close to, or more accurately in, the office. Behind a revolving bookcase (which opens with the pull of a secret book) or accessible from a separate private entrance, is another world complete with bedroom, library,

outdoor space, and luxurious master bath. The library and the bedroom are separated by four massive floor-to-ceiling bookcases that pivot closed, allowing the use of the library as a second bedroom. A wall of closets and a two-way mirror separate the master bath and the master bedroom, while allowing light from the 10-foot windows to enter into the tub and shower area. A custom glass-enclosed Murphy bed, another Arts Corporation sculpture, completes the space.

4

5

6

Appliances
New York, New York

1

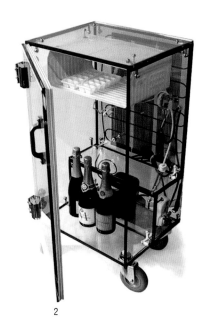

2

1 espresso.alarm, 2005 (glass, electronics, and hardware, 14" x 12" x 12") **2** RE.frigerator, 2004, (glass, electronics, and hardware – wine not included, 34" x 18' x 16") **3** T.DVD, 2004, (glass, electronics, and hardware) **4** T.VCR, 2004 (glass, electronics, and hardware. 24" x 24' x 16") **5** 5.CD.player, 2004 (glass, electronics, and hardware. 3' x 16" x 10") **6** Detail of 5.CD.player, showing holes for speakers mounted behind **Jen Campbell; Vikram Gandhi; Richard Prince**

This series of sculptures questions the utility and mass-manufactured nature of common household objects, in varied edition numbers. These appliances are one-of-a-kind, immaculately crafted sculptures inspired by objects from everyday American life. The espresso.alarm was commissioned in a very limited-edition run by the editors of the premier edition of *Men's Vogue*. The edition was also sponsored by Tiffany and Co., which supplied the Atlas® alarm clock. When the alarm rings, it triggers the integral espresso machine to brew a cup of espresso. Other works express the intricacies of their mechanical workings, freed from the shroud of the anonymous plastic or metal that typically obscures the life inside the box. Many of the appliances are designed to move around a space, commanding territory wherever their wheels take them.

3

5

4

6

1 Access is gained through a built-in ladder **2** The top of the unit offers a place to sleep **3** Home.in.1 is a self-contained object sheathed in translucent glass **4** Translucent glass doors open to reveal a compact world inside **Andrew Bordwin**

Home.in.1
New York, New York

Home.in.1 had a limited budget for the creation of storage space and furniture—a bed, bookshelves, and a desk—in a New York studio apartment. The solution conflates the furniture program and the client's possessions into a mobile 6-foot cube, or "pixel," made of standard 1.25-inch shelving angles, glass, and acrylic. In its location as photographed, the result is a high level of openness and organization in a space that might otherwise be overwhelmed by objects. Home.in.1, and its contents, can be moved against a wall allowing for open studio workspace. The unit can be disassembled and reassembled by two people in two days of work.

1

2

3

4

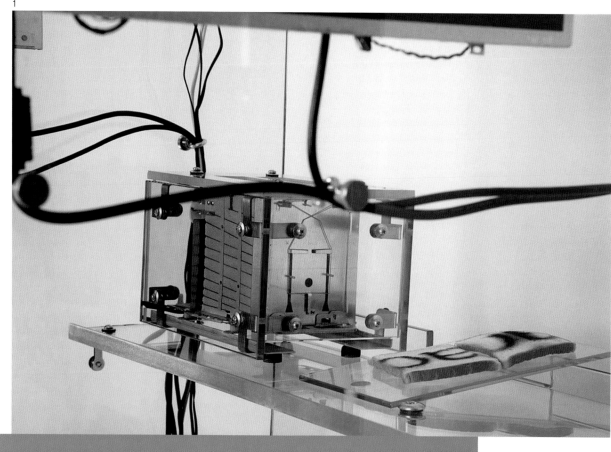

1

T.oaster kiosk
New York, New York

Contemporary art fair Pulse New York 2008 commissioned an installation built around the Arts Corporation t.oaster. The original and generative work, the t.oaster, consists simply of the ubiquitous American toaster, in this case a finely crafted glass box constructed along the lines of other Arts Corporation "inventions," with the Arts Corporation's logo etched into the surface.

The kiosk takes the form of a glass booth in the center of the fair, along the lines of the typology of the pavilions in American shopping malls that sell anything from candy to sunglasses. In this case the kiosk is selling art in the middle of an art fair. While video screens alternate between projections of short informational videos explaining how to use the t.oaster and photographic stills of the work, which are also available as prints, scrolling signs announce the name of the work and its price.

Meanwhile, on the inside, four Arts Corporation "ambassadors," women cast for their similar appearance and virtually unintelligible English, interact with the public using only lines from the informational video. They are dressed in custom Arts Corporation uniforms, embroidered with the Arts Corporation logo and the various brand marks of the t.oaster, also evident on the t.oaster's box, which sits in the rear of the booth. At set intervals during the day, they hand out business cards with their names on them, and demonstrate the use of the t.oaster, which duly burns the Arts Corporation logo into every piece of toast.

In this way, the original, small sculptural work enlarges its own meaning, generating the creation of a body of work including work on paper, photographs, video, costume, installation, and performance.

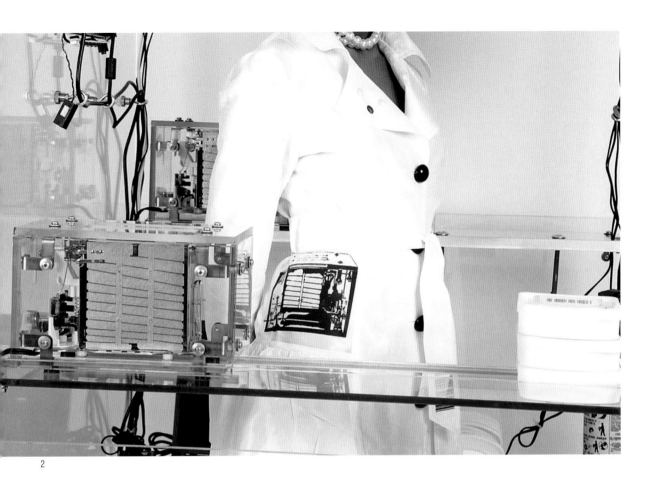

2

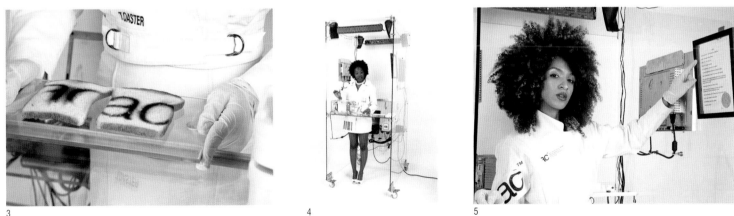

3

4

5

1 Detail of t.oaster and its products **2** Detail of the kiosk t.oaster with ambassador nearby **3** Bread is toasted with the Arts Corporation logo **4** One of the four ambassadors in the kiosk **5** A warranty is included in the kiosk **Jen Campbell**

Christoff:Finio Architecture

250 West Broadway, 4th Floor, New York, New York, 10013 212.219.1026

www.christofffinio.com

STRUCTURE MATTER FORM RITUAL TIME SPACE

WHO WE ARE:
Taryn Christoff, Martin Finio

OUR ARCHITECTURAL VALUES IN A DOZEN WORDS:
clarity; restraint; ambiguity; economy; intelligence; performance; abstraction; construction; collaboration; connection; place; presence

OUR ARCHITECTURAL PHILOSOPHY IN THREE-DOZEN WORDS:
Architecture is less a product than a way of thinking.

Architecture is a disciplined approach to the context of human activity.

Architecture is elusive and therefore worth searching for.

Architecture takes time. And patience. And practice.

OUR PRACTICE IN 20-DOZEN WORDS:

"No ideas but in things" is a line from a poem by William Carlos Williams—an American poet and key member of the early Modernist movement. The line is a reaction by Williams against other poets of his time, like Pound and Eliot, who, in his opinion, relied too heavily on connections to sources that were so elusive and so arcane that their work became inaccessible.

Williams worked from what he called *the local*. He was interested in what was right in front of him. This, to him, was important and complex enough.

We have similar sympathies. We work with the problem that is in front of us.

This is not an argument for contextualism. We are not promoting narrow mindedness or provincialism. And we are certainly not arguing against intellectualism. This is an argument for taking what you think you know, and what you think of as familiar to you, and looking at it very hard, so that it becomes *un*familiar, and new, and therefore beautiful, and worth reckoning with.

We work to make a problem strong and clear, so that those who work with us can see the problem too, and can use their particular skills to help us create a strong and clear response to it. We think of ourselves as problem solvers, and therefore look at any problem of space, time, matter, money, infrastructure, or organization as architecture, and therefore solvable.

FREQUENT COLLABORATORS:

Buro Happold Engineers
Brooklyn Digital Foundry
Everyone who has passed through our studio

WHY WE PRACTICE IN NEW YORK IN TWO-DOZEN WORDS:

Physical, intellectual, and cultural density. It's a small miracle that every morning, New York wakes up, turns on the faucet, and water comes out.

Aqua Center
Aalborg, Denmark

This competition design includes swimmers and spectators as equal participants in a structure that seeks to redefine how we relate to water in a constructed environment. A series of concrete ribbons repeat over the distance of the poolroom, serving at one scale as a form through which water may be cradled, islands may be formed, beaches may emerge, bridges may span, and diving platforms may rise. At a more intimate scale, surfaces respond directly to the size and shape of the human body, folding or stretching as needed to form ways in and out of the water as well as places to sit or recline in and around the water, and connecting to other spaces within the building. A required "circuit" pool is implied by the bends and folds of adjacent slabs. The overall impression is one of an undulating interior landscape that offers infinite possibilities for interactions between people and water.

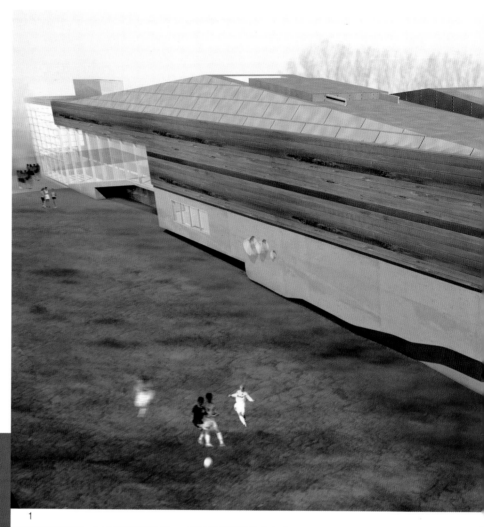

1

2

3

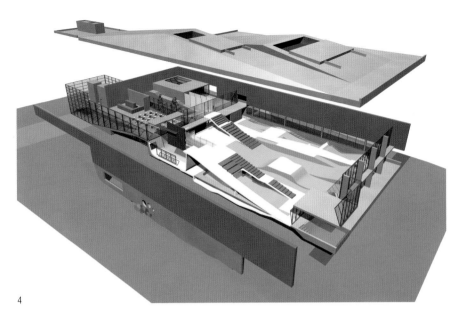

4

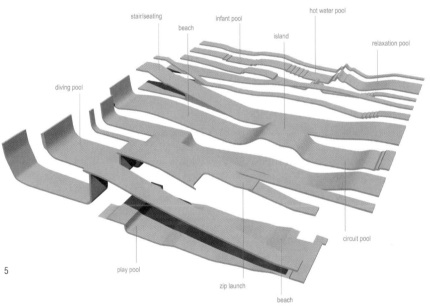

stair/seating
beach
infant pool
island
hot water pool
relaxation pool
diving pool
circuit pool
5
play pool
zip launch
beach

1 The exterior echoes the undulations of the pool's ribbons **2** Long view of the various pools and places to relax **3** Pools are defined by concrete ribbons and glass **4** Exploded view of the Aqua Center complex **5** Diagram of the poolroom's undulating concrete ribbons

Carriage House
New York, New York

The original 19th-century carriage house on this site in New York City's West Village had been through many adaptations in its lifetime, including the addition of a Moorish façade in the 1970s. In 2006 it was significantly damaged by fire and had to be rebuilt. Its small (20-foot-by-28-foot) footprint and two-story limitation offered an opportunity to re-imagine the potential for a modest urban dwelling in the city.

The house sits directly behind a large townhouse on the same lot occupied by the owner. His intention was to rebuild the damaged property as a private residence to let. The new house is entered from a 15-foot-wide cobblestone alley through an ornamental metal screenwall. Immediately behind this screen is a shallow, covered outdoor space. This narrow sliver of real estate serves as a compressed, urban version of a garage, perfect for bicycle, motorbike, or recycling storage.

At the opposite end of the house, a small rear terrace extends the kitchen and living areas outdoors. Windows on this side are kept low to the ground to maintain privacy from the back of the abutting townhouse, just 12 feet away. The rear elevation is comprised of 3-foot-long cleft slate shingles. Two small bedrooms and a bathroom make up the top floor, where a large skylight over the stairwell floods both levels with daylight.

The house sits tucked behind several taller towers (among them works by Richard Meier and Asymptote). Its green roof offers visual relief to the many inhabitants above, as well as a habitat for birds and other animals.

1

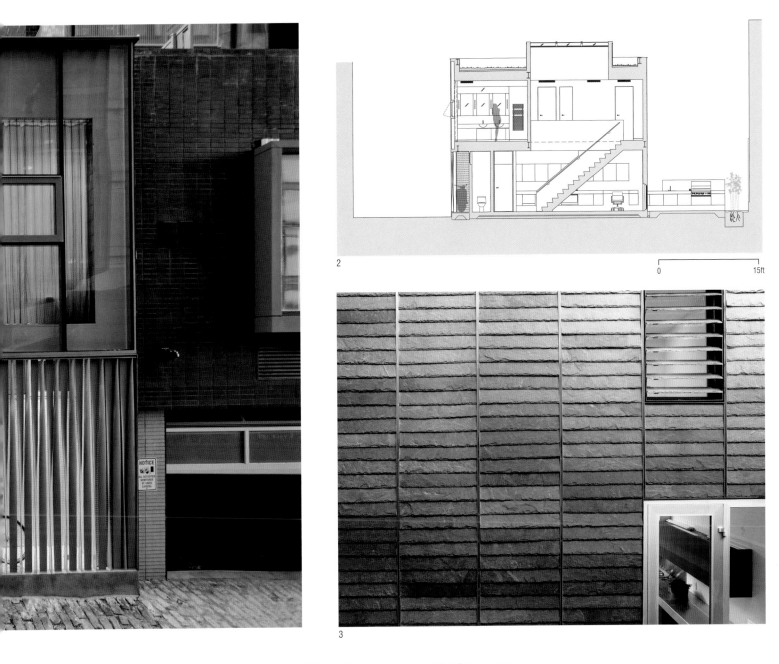

1 Entry façade 2 Section 3 Slate shingles clad the rear elevation **Jan Staller**

Section drawing scale
0   15ft

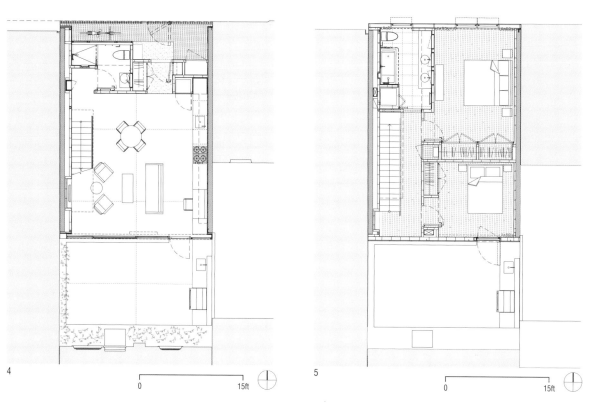

4

0   15ft

5

0   15ft

6

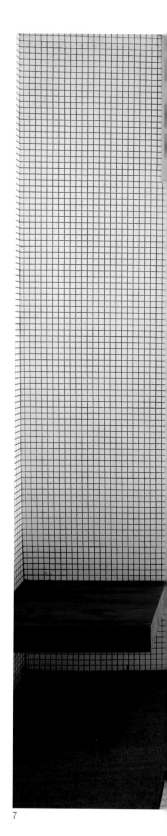

7

4 First floor plan **5** Second floor plan **6** Ground level stair **7** "Urban garage" behind screen wall
8 Interior/exterior view **9** Section **Jan Staller**

8

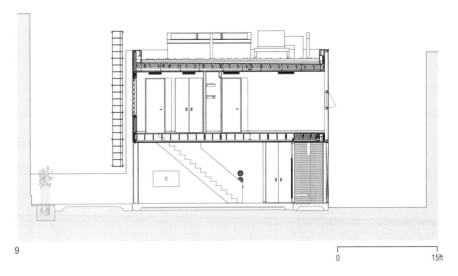

9

0 ⊢————————————⊣ 15ft

Heckscher Foundation Headquarters
New York, New York

1 The exterior of the classically designed façade **opposite** View of the expanding space from the entry **Elizabeth Felicella**

Commissioned by the Heckscher Foundation for Children, this project transforms a stoic neo-Georgian townhouse built in 1902 in New York City into a modern interior for the foundation's administration, providing offices, a boardroom, and small conference spaces. The goal of this project was to fundamentally redefine the traditional townhouse interior and thereby infuse both the foundation and its building with new relevance.

By incising a shaft of daylight from the rooftop to the ground floor, the organization of the building's activity is centered on a single gesture of light and space. Floor plates are pulled away from one supporting wall, their weight suspended by steel rods connected from a single point in the roof, articulating the bold gesture of the void. By relieving the wall and ground plane of traditional supportive elements, the huge glass volume of the offices overhead appears to hover weightlessly above the ground plane. Preserved elements from the original townhouse, such as elaborate wood windows, gilt-framed portraits, and ornamental fireplaces, are highlighted by the sharp lines of the zebrawood paneling and graphic effect of the white steel and glass that create a playful and dynamic juxtaposition of time and place.

The transformation of a building whose full horizontal and vertical interior dimension is now experienced upon entry yields a space that maintains its domestic scale while simultaneously addressing the larger scale of the overall building site.

3 Section **4** Reception desk and bench **5** Boardroom and upper floors suspended above entry **6** Detail of glass-enclosed stair **7** Lightshaft, with suspended space to the left **Elizabeth Felicella**

3

4

5

6

7

Museum as Hub
New Museum of Contemporary Art
New York, New York

Museum as Hub is a new programmatic initiative run by the New Museum of Contemporary Art, coinciding with the opening of their new home on the Bowery in New York City. The Hub concept reflects the recognition that contemporary art is defined globally, and that any organization devoted to it must find inventive ways to sustain the complex exchange between artists, institutions, and the public on an international level. Museum as Hub is therefore a cultural laboratory, exploring art and ideas through a new global partnership between the New Museum and, in this introductory year, four other partners in Seoul, Cairo, Eindhoven, and Mexico City. Together these partners will program the fifth-floor Education Center in the New Museum's new facility on the Bowery.

The design was selected through an invited competition, sponsored by the museum, to give physical presence to the Hub's mission within the fifth-floor shell of the museum (partitions, lighting, and MEP were pre-established in the museum's design).

This solution seeks to distill the Hub concept to its essence. Through a most reductive palette of table, chair, and curtain—and the interaction between them—the Hub manages to operate at many scales, and accommodates (and contests) many different agendas. This is a shifting space for one and for many, where two people or 20 people (or 20 million via computer screens) can engage in the exchange of ideas through a very simple act: coming to the table.

1 Tables and curtains can be deployed to configure an infinite number of spatial possibilities within the structured logic of their tracks 2 Table legs index to form connected surfaces 3 Publications are displayed near the computer terminals 4 View of the Hub's library 5 Curtains provide flexibility, scale, color, and texture

Christopher Lovi

4

5

Napeague House
Long Island, New York

1

The seemingly limitless possibilities for building on this undeveloped stretch of oceanfront dune belie the complicated zoning restrictions that encumber it. A sensitivity to both the natural conditions of the site and the building codes placed upon it led to the formation of an elevated, double-bar building connected at the upper level by a transparent glass bridge, and at grade by a stone terrace and lap pool.

A sawtooth profile complies with the enforced requirement of a sloped roof, while also providing optimum conditions for south-facing photovoltaic panels and north-facing skylights. The high output panels will generate approximately 27 kilowatt hours, enough to power the entire house, including heating the pool. Coupled with a geothermal cooling system, radiant floor heating, high-performance glass coatings, and a revegetation plan that will restore the landscape to its original condition, the project spares no effort to tread lightly on the land. Its impact on the site will be equivalent to a house a small fraction of its size. While houses in the Hamptons will most likely not be shrinking anytime soon, we can (and should) design them to perform as if they were.

2

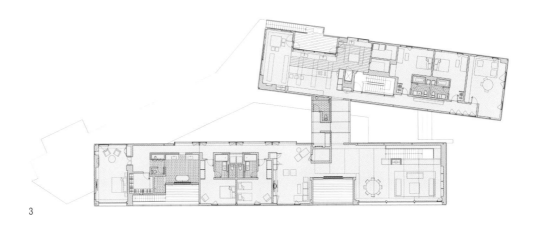

3

1 Glass entry from the deck
2 View from the bridge
3 Second floor plan 4 First
floor plan 5 View of the
living/dining area with its
variegated roof that admits
light 6 Living/dining area
Brooklyn Digital Foundry

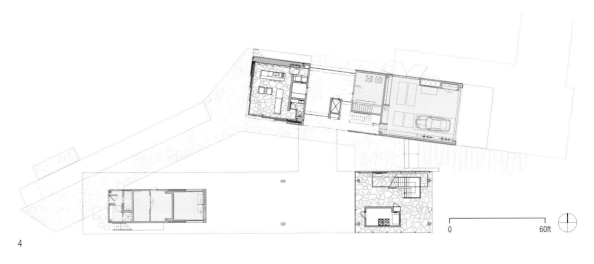

4

0   60ft

5   6

World Trade Center Memorial Proposal

New York, New York

1

The foundation of this proposal is a new layer of urban infrastructure that would reinvent the New York City skyline: a "farm" of wind turbines that would gradually spread across the rooftops of the city, standing as the silent witnesses to our loss and as the symbolic divestment of our dependence on foreign oil. The turbines' rotating arms would shape a public space of memory far beyond the confines of the World Trade Center site, generating physical and emotional energy from the same wind that keeps planes aloft, carries clouds of debris, fuels fires, and sustains life.

The proposal states that the New York City Zoning Resolution be amended to require all residential and commercial buildings over a certain gross area to generate a percentage of their own electrical consumption using rooftop wind turbines that harness the power of prevailing winds. The percentage would be determined as a factor of the building's size and use. For practical reasons, these requirements would be phased in over the course of several years.

2

3

1 Timeline of the World Trade Center Memorial Proposal
2 Downtown turbines as seen from the Empire State Building
3 The implementation of the proposed zoning amendment would happen over the course of several years to allow the retrofitting of existing buildings to happen at a reasonable rate (view toward the northeast)

Della Valle Bernheimer

20 Jay Street, Brooklyn, New York, 11201

www.dbnyc.com

WHO WE ARE:
Jared Della Valle, Andrew Bernheimer

OUR ARCHITECTURAL VALUES IN A DOZEN WORDS:
Pragmatism, Rigor, Forthrightness, Legibility, Depth, Texture, Self-reliance, Calibration, Surprise, Ingenuity, Newness, Clarity.

OUR ARCHITECTURAL PHILOSOPHY IN THREE-DOZEN WORDS:
Our diverse practice is rooted in an ongoing effort to invent and formulate projects for ourselves and to create a world where others may also live. We create projects with the intention of surprising our clients.

New York offers an engaging community of practitioners and builders who are willing to connect and help execute our design concepts in practical terms.

OUR PRACTICE IN 20-DOZEN WORDS:

Our buildings, like those of most architects, are effectively the first and last of their kind. Usually, they are made by proven methodologies that have been tested internally; however, unless deployed in a repeated fashion, each project is a one-off, never rebuilt. We aim to mitigate risk by a reduction of systems, through stringent research into new methods of fabrication beyond the common, and through the simplification of architectural language. After the initial moment of instinct, we think through ways of making, while intellectual and mechanical mental associations play crucial roles.

We also search for a "distillation of thought," which we believe makes spaces and designs accessible and enriching—even if our intentions are not, on the surface, legible to others. Everyone's intuition is different, but if the design is well articulated, we can enter each other's thought-spaces. Our architecture is a kind of syllogism, where primary elements and secondary textures combine, legibly and intuitively, to guide users to their own distinctive and diverse responses.

We have thought through the business side of our impulses, and this has allowed us, as practitioners, to proactively expand the rules of development within our firm. We strive to always think anew—to make each project unlike any that preceded it. The absence of an overarching signature is not an earth-shattering pronouncement on our part; rather, it liberates us. We believe in consistency, not homogeneity. We seek to make things that are thoughtful, interpretive, and substantial.

FREQUENT COLLABORATORS:

Nat Oppenheimer, Robert Silman Associates Engineers
Guy Nordenson and Brett Schneider, Guy Nordenson Associates
Mike Ra, FRONT

23 Beekman Place
New York, New York

Built in 1978, Paul Rudolph's penthouse apartment and office at 23 Beekman Place has become an icon for this legendary architect's distinctive ideas about form, materials, and lifestyle. Rudolph maintained the apartment as an ongoing experiment until his death in 1997, relentlessly altering its design and ultimately creating a series of many projects in one home.

In 2004 Della Valle Bernheimer was asked by the new owner to restore and update the penthouse. Previous renovations completed after Rudolph's death were unsympathetic to the original, with a recent renovation having been halted midstream with only demolition and plumbing rough-in completed. The new owner wanted to modernize the apartment and, despite the lack of a single historic design reference, the firm took on the daunting task of creating the contemporary progeny of Rudolph's designs. In-depth documentation of previous design iterations, along with the rigorous examination and understanding of Rudolph's design principles, resulted in a re-interpretation rather than a traditional renovation. The resulting design is an extrapolation of how Paul Rudolph might have continued his experiments—given modern innovations and new technology.

1

1 Exterior view **2** View from entrance **3** Stair, rail, and skylight detail **4** Acrylic and glass floors along with transparent handrails and reflective surfaces give a vertiginous sense to the apartment **5** Stairway intersection with structure and window **Richard Barnes**

2

3

4

5

459 West 18th Street

New York, New York

1

Della Valle Bernheimer acted as both architect and developer of this residential project located between two vibrant and evolving neighborhoods—the Meatpacking District and Chelsea—on the west side of Manhattan. On the edge of what once was the shoreline of Manhattan, the bold design for this mixed-use condominium project appears resolutely within its context. Severe in mass and profile, the confident exterior of the tower belies its carefully muted interiors. The building envelope is comprised of composite panels and white and clear glass. Fenestration punctures through the building mass are expressed as extruded collars. In an effort to blur the delineation between interior and exterior, and to eliminate the distraction of mullions typically associated with curtain wall systems, massive expanses of glass add a cinematic quality, framing views like art-in-progress. Meticulously designed details and thoughtfully selected materials achieve an understated, serene interior that is in marked contrast to the rigorously prominent building exterior and the neighborhood.

2

1 View from the High Line at night **2** Dormer at penthouse terrace **3** Typical living room **4** Penthouse living room **Frank Oudeman, BLiP Studio**

3

4

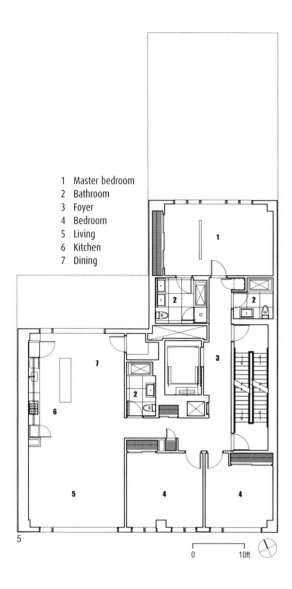

1 Master bedroom
2 Bathroom
3 Foyer
4 Bedroom
5 Living
6 Kitchen
7 Dining

5

0   10ft

5 Typical floor plan **6** Penthouse dining room **BLiP Studio; Della Valle Bernheimer**

6

Butterfly Pavilion
Philbrook Museum of Art
Tulsa, Oklahoma

1

2

This design for a garden structure at the Philbrook Museum of Art originates in the spirit and etymology of the word "pavilion," which is derived from the French "papillon," meaning butterfly. The cocoon-like Butterfly Pavilion is also inspired by the entomological transformation of the silkworm into the butterfly. In an act of becoming, the silkworm pupates, spinning itself an intricate chamber.

The Butterfly Pavilion resembles a cocoon, not spun of silk but etched and cut from plate steel. Using laser cutting technology, a diminutive 8-foot-by-16-foot pavilion was fabricated from wood decking and steel tubes. Two layers of quarter-inch-thick panels, powder-coated in white (the outside layer) and sky blue (the inside layer) are attached to the steel structure. Etched into these panels is the repeated and abstracted pattern of a butterfly that filters light and creates an artificial cocoon, perfect as a contemplative space for one. Light passing through these patterned walls creates a latticework of dappled light and shadow, providing the visitor with transformative solitude while maintaining a gentle visual connection to the museum grounds. At night, the pavilion transforms, becoming a lantern that casts a soft, diffused glow.

3

4

5

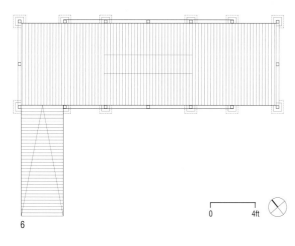

6

1 Butterfly outline **2** Interior view at night **3** Exterior view at night **4** Pavilion interior **5** View through pavilion skin **6** Pavilion plan **Della Valle Bernheimer**

Copper House
Hudson Valley, New York

The Copper House is located in the Hudson Valley on a wooded, 6-acre site two hours north of New York City. Clad almost entirely in corrugated copper siding and a mixture of flat-seam and standing-seam copper roofing, the skin will age and develop a patina reflecting time through material changes. The three-bedroom house features distinctive, sculpted south-facing skylights that allow light into various public and private spaces.

The ground floor contains two bedrooms, a living room, dining room, kitchen, and a home office. An 8-foot-tall, 30-foot-long, open bookshelf system runs the length of the ground floor, creating a sense of delineation between rooms while retaining visual connections across the various spaces. The second floor contains a master bedroom, playroom, and attic space, with windows overlooking the sculpted copper skylights.

1

1 Southwest view at dusk 2 North façade 3 The protruding cedar box is a home office **Richard Barnes**

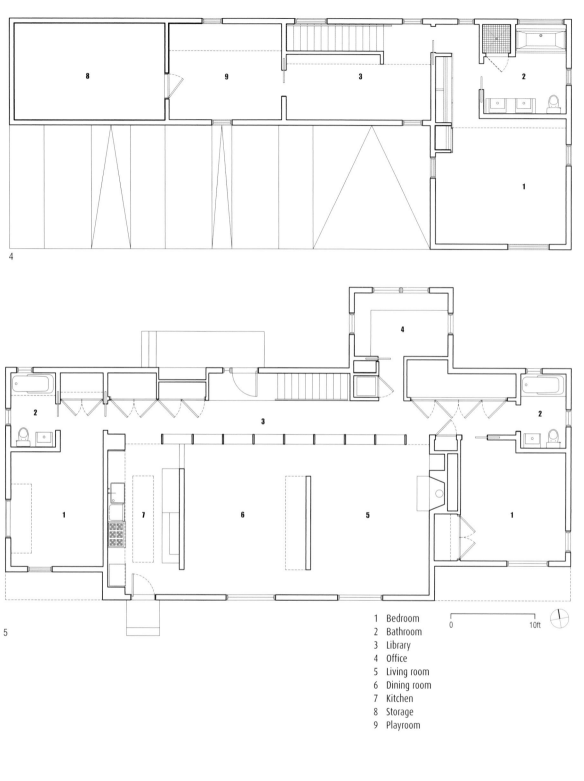

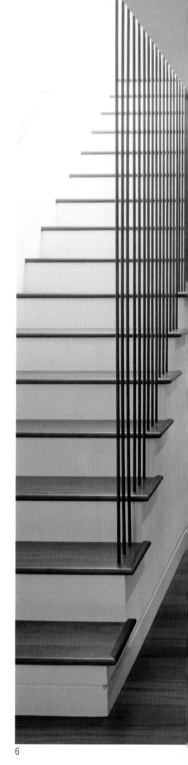

1 Bedroom
2 Bathroom
3 Library
4 Office
5 Living room
6 Dining room
7 Kitchen
8 Storage
9 Playroom

0   10ft

4 Second floor plan **5** Ground floor plan **6** Hallway and stairwell **7** Master bathroom **8** Guest bedroom **Richard Barnes**

1

2

706.5 SF   383 SF

1 View from rear yard at night **2** Floor plans **3** View from stairwell **4** Model photo **DB & ARO**

R-HOUSE
Syracuse, New York

This prototype residence presents an affordable, innovative paradigm for minimal energy consumption embodied in architecture that nurtures the spirit and engages the community. Framed within its iconic exterior are expansive and luminous spaces that require only the equivalent energy of a hair dryer for heating. Its efficient plan can be tailored to meet the needs of different families and is readily adapted as these needs change over time. Designed for high economic and practical performance, R-House strengthens the physical and social structure of the Near Westside neighborhood.

R-House transforms a typical gabled roof into a simply folded surface that recalls the appearance and scale of neighboring houses. Tucked within the house are a front porch and rear deck whose translucent walls cast an inviting glow after dark. Windows and skylights open the interior to views and are optimized to receive south light. The roof and walls are sheathed with corrugated aluminum. The silver color, muted reflectivity, and fine texture of this cladding contribute to a sense of vibrancy that counters the gray winter months.

A two-story space on the south side of the house, lit by large windows that open to a view of the rear yard, is bounded by the stairwell and the master bedroom on the second floor. Humble, carefully detailed materials such as concrete, wood floor boards, and plywood panels imbue the home with warmth and integrity. Translucent polycarbonate panels cover the east wall of the bedrooms, creating a soft, luminous boundary between the private and public areas of the house. The stair rail and kitchen island, made from the same material, are backlit to illuminate the interior.

The design meets the German Passivhaus ultra-low energy standard, which utilizes an extremely well-insulated exterior, airtight construction, an efficient heating system, controlled ventilation, and windows that optimize solar gain. Sustainable construction materials are used throughout the house. This project was designed in collaboration with Architecture Research Office.

3

4

Leroy Street Studio

113 Hester Street, Chinatown, Lower East Side, New York, New York

www.leroystreetstudio.com

WHO WE ARE:
Tim Campbell, Christine Chang, Julie Fisher, Morgan Hare, Greg Heasley, Katice Helinski, Sebastijan Jemec, Arom Jeon, Laura Reneke, Pauline Shu, Lesli Stinger, Younglan Tsai, Marc Turkel (Partner), Shawn Watts (Partner)

OUR ARCHITECTURAL VALUES IN A DOZEN WORDS:
To build intelligent, efficient, and engaging environments that are rooted in relationships.

TO COLLABORATE, TO INNOVATE, TO BUILD.

OUR ARCHITECTURAL PHILOSOPHY IN THREE-DOZEN WORDS:
The art of architecture has a collaborative heart. As architects we layer viewpoints and responses by focusing intent, expertise, and talent. We frame new opportunities and solutions by combining landscape, structure, enclosure, building systems, and materials.

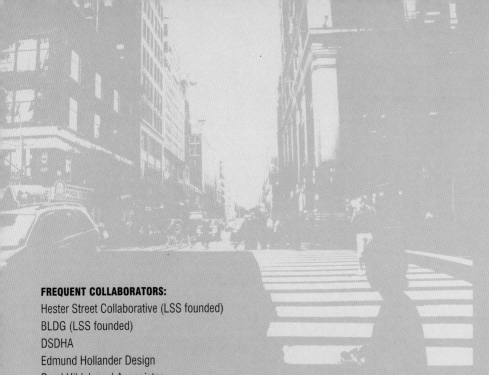

FREQUENT COLLABORATORS:

Hester Street Collaborative (LSS founded)

BLDG (LSS founded)

DSDHA

Edmund Hollander Design

Reed Hildebrand Associates

Dlandstudio

Blue Sky Design

Robert Silman Associates

Atelier Ten

Right Environments

Buro Happold Consulting Engineers

Tripower Engineering

Clinard Design Studio

Isometrix

Lighting Design International

Veere Grenney Associates

Ingrao, Inc.

Bruce Bierman Design

KA Design Group

Thad Hayes

PS New York

Pentagram

Partnerships for Parks

Robin Hood Foundation

Asian Americans for Equality

WHY WE PRACTICE IN NEW YORK IN TWO-DOZEN WORDS:

New York trains architects to respond to the needs of this century: living in dense cities, lifting lives through design, and creating healthy communities.

OUR PRACTICE IN 20-DOZEN WORDS:

Today's environmental, economic, and practical challenges demand a deep understanding and constant rethinking of conventional design solutions and methodologies. To create innovative solutions for each project's unique issues and often-contradictory goals, LSS examines each architectural program in its physical, cultural, economic, and environmental context. Our process of research, exploration, and synthesis has led us to explore alternative approaches to design, client relationships, and project delivery.

Our work is borne out of the art of building with an awareness of the latest building technologies and the realities of the building industry. Through this lens we explore the qualities of structure, space, form, materials, light, and landscape at every stage of a project's development. LSS founded the construction-management firm BLDG to allow the studio to get closer to the construction process and provide alternative solutions cost-effectively.

We cultivate an inclusive design process that meaningfully engages clients, design professionals, artists, builders, and craftspeople through all stages of the project. Partners and studio members work as a team to refine and test solutions. We work across project types and scales and have developed methods for offering services to those who are typically left out of the process of making cities and buildings. As a natural extension of our design process we formed Hester Street Collaborative—a nonprofit organization that practices design activism: empowering local community members to participate in envisioning, designing, and building elements that improve streets, playgrounds, housing projects, community centers, and schools.

Louver House

Designed for a client with a passion for barns, this project seeks to capture the qualities of traditional barn structures (generous spaces and repetitive timber frames), while developing a modern building responding to the demands both of a residential program, and a site's dramatic views. Sited on the edge of an open agricultural reserve, the house's public spaces are elevated to the second floor to capture the long views. To unify the various internal and external spaces, a translucent wrapper for the building was designed, fabricated of timber louvers and rain-screen siding. In all, five outdoor courts and garden spaces are unified under a single roof, giving the structure a double reading of complexity up close, yet simple and monolithic from afar.

1 View from the south at night showing solid and void space behind the wood-louvered skin **2** Section **3** View through louvered screen to the glass-enclosed entry vestibule **4** View from southeast **Paul Warchol**

The entry sequence draws one through the building's louvered skin into a two-story foyer overlooking a three-story interior garden courtyard. A ceiling-scape of delicate three-dimensional trussed timber and steel members unifies the upper spaces: a large hall with kitchen, dining, and living functions, a large outdoor porch, a garden mezzanine, and a study. A stone fireplace and chimney offers an asymmetrical counterpoint and opens onto both the interior and exterior space.

3

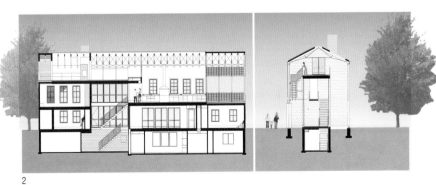

2

4

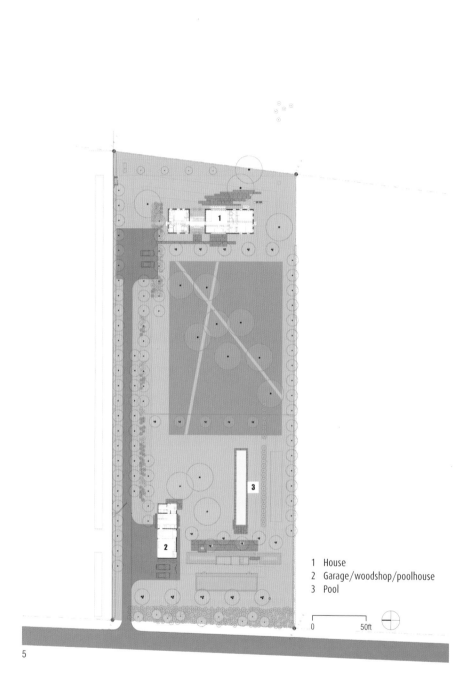

5

6

7

8

1 House
2 Garage/woodshop/poolhouse
3 Pool

0   50ft

5 Site plan **6** Roof trusses and spine skylight **7** Entry vestibule and stair hall **8** View from northeast: folding doors allow the landscape to flow through the building at ground floor **9** Main living space from porch with exterior attic porch beyond **10** Main-floor elevated porch with operable louver panels **11** Stainless steel 3D truss connector **Leroy Street Studio; Paul Warchol Photography**

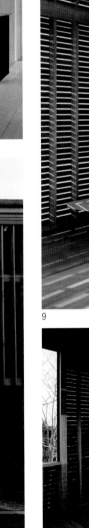

9

10

11

STONE HOUSES
Long Island, New York

1

2

3

4

For a very flat, 12-acre site dotted with specimen trees, a mother and daughter requested a low-maintenance weekend residence of Westchester granite for themselves and their extended family. The property was planned as two separate houses linked with a network of dry-stack stone walls that create a solid and private face at the southern-oriented arrival side of the buildings. The walls unify exterior and interior spaces and knit the buildings together resulting in a series of internal and external courtyard spaces. Floating roofs define living spaces and great expanses of glazing open toward views of the agricultural reserve to the north.

The first house, House One, has a slot of water that cuts through the courtyard wall to mark the entry, which is accessed through an oversized cabinet that pierces the forecourt curtain wall. A long gallery runs east–west along one of the walls and links the public and private wings. A glass bridge cuts across the gallery linking two ends of an elevated guest wing.

The second house, House Two, is entered at its narrowest point, through a glazed hall overlooking a raised garden court. A series of floating roofs connects the entry to the interior and exterior public spaces—all nestled against the stone walls. The private wing is defined, in contrast, as a taut box of oak Glulam portal frames wrapped in a continuous skin of louvers.

1 House One is entered through the forecourt defined by stone walls **2** Forecourt of House One viewed from the east **3** Stone wall passes through House One to define entry gallery **4** House One: view from north **5** House One: glass bridge connects guest rooms across main gallery space below **6** House One plan **Leroy Street Studio; Paul Warchol Photography**

6

0   10ft

5

8

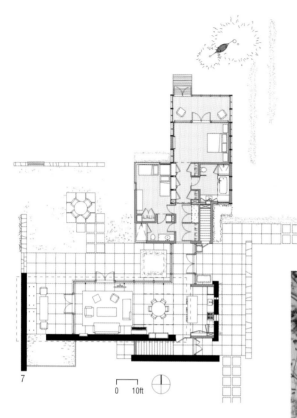

7

0   10ft

9

10

7 House Two plan **8** House Two windows illuminate kitchen beyond **9** Covered exterior court of House Two with water feature **10** House Two: view from northeast with mother's house beyond **11** House Two main living space defined by wood curtain wall, stone wall, and floating roofs. Kitchen is beyond. **Leroy Street Studio; Paul Warchol Photography**

11

Architecture Office
New York, New York

1

Housed in a former tablecloth factory, these offices were built by BLDG—the construction management wing of Leroy Street Studio. Taking into consideration the context of Chinatown and the Lower East Side, Leroy Street Studio developed an unassuming yet expressive and welcoming presence on the block. Hester Street Collaborative (the nonprofit community design wing of the firm) has its workshop in the storefront. The interior of the building was extended and skylights were added for natural light. Below the largest skylight a suspended steel stair links the two floors of the architecture studio.

For cost control, off-the-shelf elements are used throughout the project in unconventional ways. For example, steel floor joists are suspended with steel cables and repurposed as shelving and extruded polycarbonate panels give privacy to the workstations and conference room while allowing light through. The architect experimented with dyes and stains to give depth to the low-cost fiberboard millwork throughout.

2

3

1 The entry level uses bright epoxy over the existing wood floor to reflect light throughout **2** The façade before construction **3** Upper level with steel joist shelving and millwork made of fiberboard and repurposed steel fire doors **4** Floor plans **5** Suspended stair made from off-the-shelf grating and steel cables allows light to penetrate through to below **Leroy Street Studio; Paul Warchol Photography**

4

0 5ft

5

Hester Street Collaborative
New York, New York

1

In 2001, Leroy Street Studio founded Hester Street Collaborative (HSC), a nonprofit organization that uses design as a tool for social change. HSC seeks to improve the built environment for all New Yorkers with a hands-on approach that combines design, advocacy, and education. HSC has found that there exists in low-income communities a huge demand as well as a reservoir of energy and talent for remaking public spaces—all that is lacking is the organizational and financial resources. All too often the approach is top-down without an understanding of the communities' needs.

HSC's guiding principle is that civic engagement in participatory design helps disadvantaged residents create a profound impact on their communities. HSC works with local residents to transform neglected public spaces in streets, parks, schools, and affordable housing developments through a design/build process that capitalizes on local knowledge and resources, gives stakeholders an active role, and encourages meaningful community stewardship.

Today, HSC and Leroy Street Studio work together closely on community design projects as well as design education efforts.

This partnership promotes the exchange of professional expertise between the nonprofit and professional design worlds and allows Leroy Street Studio to serve a wider audience.

1 HSC worked with local students to build the Avenue of the Immigrants installation to highlight the need for community involvement in the renovation of the Allen and Pike street malls 2 HSC served as design liaison between the Parks Department and the community and led a design–build exercise where students designed artwork installations for the SDR Park in Chinatown. The temporary lantern installation by local MS 131 students was part of the endeavor to raise awareness 3 HSC built a new outdoor science and art classroom and garden with students and teachers of PS 134 4 Leroy Street Studio and HSC formed a charrette to design and build the entry gate to the PS 134 garden. Recycled concrete slabs and student-made pavers line the path beyond **Leroy Street Studio; Hester Street Collaborative**

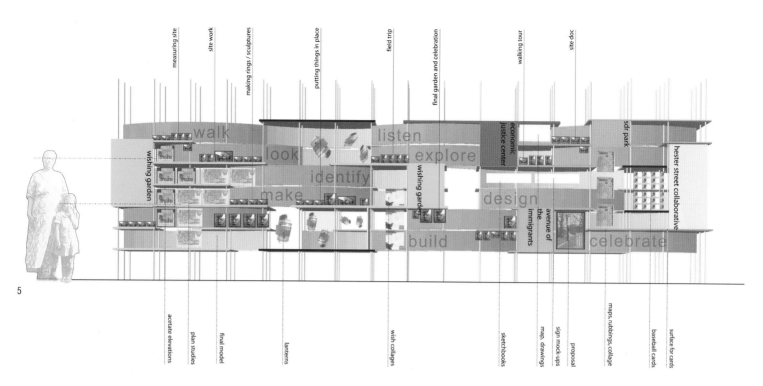

measuring site
site work
making rings / sculptures
putting things in place
field trip
final garden and celebration
walking tour
site doc

walk
look
listen
explore
identify
wishing garden
make
design
build
celebrate

wishing garden
economic justice center
avenue of the immigrants
sdr park
hester street collaborative

5

acetate elevations
plan studies
final model
lanterns
wish collages
sketchbooks
map, drawings
sign mock-ups
proposal
maps, rubbings, collage
baseball cards
surface for cards

5&8 Elevation studies for Bad Design Darts and Other Methods for Community-Led Improvement at the Municipal Art Society. Leroy Street Studio and HSC created the exhibit to focus attention on the power of participatory design in the community. **6** At PS 134 HSC and students designed and built planters, benches, pavers, and signage along with guest artists and teachers. HSC wove the design process into the science and art curriculum **7** Leroy Street Studio and HSC worked with students, teachers, and guest artists at MS 131 to build the Wishing Garden in a derelict exterior space **9** View of Municipal Art Society installation **Leroy Street Studio**

6

7

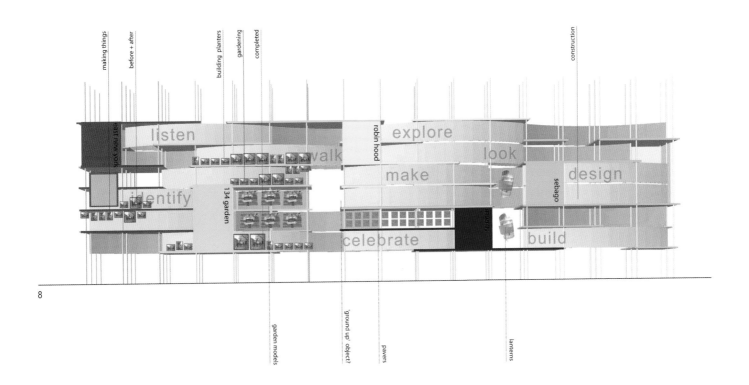

making things
before + after
building planters
gardening
completed
construction

listen
east new york
explore
robin hood
walk
look
make
identify
134 garden
sebago
design
celebrate
build

garden models
'ground up' object?
pavers
lanterns

8

9

PS 110 AND 31 LIBRARIES
New York, New York

1 Entry portal features backlit student artwork **2** Leroy Street Studio, Hester Street Collaborative, and students developed a printmaking technique to create artwork inspired by books from the collection **3** View from entry at PS 31 **4** Plan of PS 31 showing flexible classroom space, computer niche, reading ramp, and amphitheatre **Kevin Chu + Jessica Paul; Leroy Street Studio**

1

Leroy Street Studio and Hester Street Collaborative were invited to design new libraries within two public schools: Staten Island's elementary school PS 31 and Manhattan's PS 110 on the Lower East Side. The Robin Hood Foundation's Library Initiative sponsors new state-of-the-art libraries in New York City's most needy elementary schools to both engage and inspire students, and to create facilities within public schools that are accessible to the neighborhood to promote community interaction.

These state-of-the-art public school libraries were created by combining adjacent classrooms on a very modest budget. Leroy Street Studio worked as a team with not only the school administration and Robin Hood Foundation facilitators, but also with the primary users: the students. Workshops were conducted by Hester Street Collaborative, in which artworks inspired by books from the library's new collection were created. The students' work was later installed with backlighting in the library's entry portals. From there, the work became the point of departure for the color, lighting, millwork, and furnishings featured in the space.

The functional challenge was to create visually open environments, each with distinct requirements: quiet areas for reading, computer terminals, and study; open teaching and group reading areas; as well as book circulation, re-shelving, and storage zones. A line of suspended bookshelves the length of the library sets off a ramped amphitheater-like reading area from the quiet zones. The custom shelving system was perforated with large circular apertures to maintain the librarians' line of sight. Custom pentagonal tables snake through the space, allowing for flexible reconfigurations to accommodate the different requirements of each class. Off-the-shelf lighting fixtures were ringed with painted metal baffles to further echo the student's circular artwork.

2

3

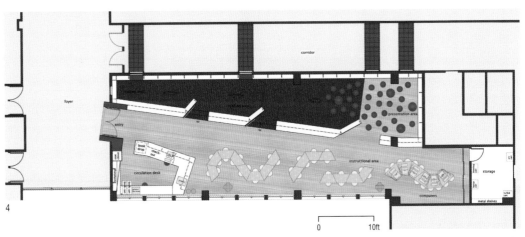

4

5

5 Suspended light fixtures echo student artwork and unify various program zones within the library **6** Ramp provides engaging and intimate reading space. Cutouts in shelving allow supervision from the librarians' station **Peter Mauss/Esto**

6

LEVENBETTS

508 W 26 St #317 New York, NY 10001

www.levenbetts.com

WHO WE ARE:
David Leven and Stella Betts

OUR ARCHITECTURAL VALUES IN A DOZEN WORDS:
Greenness, Housing, Interconnection, Juiciness, Kelvin, Lightness, Mass-transit, Newness, Openness, People, Quickness, R-value

OUR ARCHITECTURAL PHILOSOPHY IN THREE-DOZEN WORDS:
Questioning, Rapid, Synthetic, Translucent, Unconstrained, Varied, Weird, X-acto, Yes, Zoomy, AlloftheAbove, Badass, Constrained, Dumb, Exquisite, Fuzzy, GoogleEarth, Humane, Informal, JackedUp, KickedBack, LateNight, Moveable, New, Observant, Pragmatic, Quantum, Rules, Subversive, Transportable, Undone, Variable, Walkable, X-tra, Yield, Zippy

Subway, TwinTowers, Urbanism, VanWyck, Westside, X-treme, YellowCabs, ZeeDimension, Architecture, BronxandBrooklyn, CentralPark, Density, Escape, Flushing, GWBridge, HudsonRiver, Infrastructure, Jets, Knicks, L.E.S., Mies, Nervi, Olmsted, Palisades

FREQUENT COLLABORATORS:

Andrew Zuckerman
Nat Oppenhiemer
Suzanne Tillotson
Taocon
Employees

TWENTY DOZEN WORDS THAT DESCRIBE OUR PRACTICE:

LEVENBETTS is an award-winning New York City-based architecture practice established in 1997 by David Leven and Stella Betts. Pragmatic and research-based, the work of LEVENBETTS comprises a wide range of project types and sizes, from large-scale public buildings and urban proposals to houses and housing, interiors, exhibitions, and furniture. The firm's design approach begins with intensive observation and analysis in order to create innovative material, technological and environmental architectural solutions that serve the specific needs of a client and the public.

David Leven is currently an Associate Professor and Director of the Graduate Architecture program at Parsons School of Constructed Environments where he teaches in the Natural Systems Studio as well as in the final year Master of Architecture Thesis Studio. He holds a Bachelor of Arts from Colgate University in Fine Art, a Master of Architecture degree from Yale University, and attended the Institute for Architecture and Urban Studies. Stella Betts teaches at Parsons and Cooper Union, is an Assistant Professor and coordinator of the thesis studio at Parsons, and teaches in the comprehensive studio in the Bachelor of Architecture program at Cooper. Stella received her Bachelor of Arts from Connecticut College in Philosophy and Fine Art and her Master of Architecture degree from Harvard's Graduate School of Design.

The firm has won several NYC AIA awards (2008, 2005, 2004, 2003), Architectural League's Young Architects Forum and Emerging Voices Awards (2009), and the Architectural Record's Design Vanguard Award (2007).

CC01 HOUSE
Columbia County, New York

1 Detail of the house from the west **2** Southeast patio **3** The house from the northwest **4** Floor plans
Michael Moran

The design of the CC01 House begins with a reading of the landscape. Long, linear grooves, formed by the dimensions of machinery, the distance between tractor wheels, and the frequency of the blades of a plow, are etched into the rolling hills from years of farming. These lines that hug the topography were developed into diagrams that inform the design of all configurations of the house—from the primary organization and form to the cladding and details of the building. Additionally, the section of the house follows the contour of the land as it steps up from east to west along the long outdoor terrace and again between the dining and living spaces of the house. In this way, the house follows the landscape and topography both in plan and in section.

The programmatic spaces are divided between two linear volumes, one wet and the other dry. The wet zone—consisting of bathrooms, kitchen, laundry, and utilities—occupies a long, thin volume; the dry zone—consisting of the living and dining rooms and bedrooms—exists in a wider volume that provides for more generous spaces. Set into the thinner volume (the wet zone), the infrastructure of water, waste, gas piping, and heat production and distribution is an attenuated network of piping and valves. The two volumes slide past one another as they follow the linear farming pattern. Inside, the 20-foot-long kitchen counter overlaps the two volumes at the ground floor, drawing together the working (wet) and living (dry) spaces.

2

3

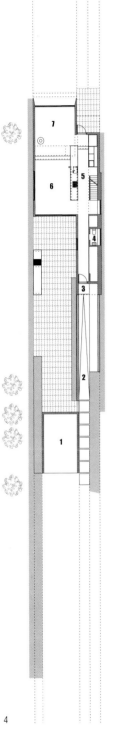

4

1 Garage
2 Entry ramp
3 Entry
4 Bathroom
5 Kitchen
6 Dining
7 Living room
8 Bedroom
9 Study

0   15ft

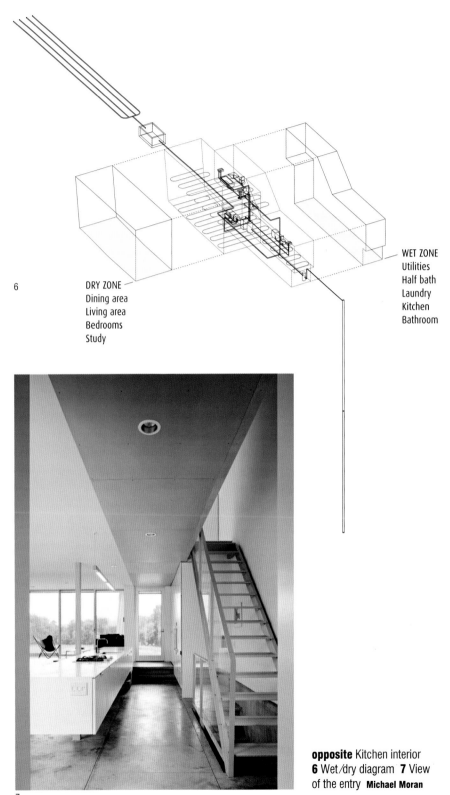

6

DRY ZONE
Dining area
Living area
Bedrooms
Study

WET ZONE
Utilities
Half bath
Laundry
Kitchen
Bathroom

opposite Kitchen interior
6 Wet/dry diagram **7** View
of the entry **Michael Moran**

7

Mixed Greens Gallery
New York, New York

1

This project for a gallery in the Chelsea art district of Manhattan includes two separate exhibition spaces, gallery offices, and storage, as well as a lounge space for browsing the gallery's online collection and hanging out during opening receptions. The space the client secured for the gallery had an irregular structural condition: a series of large wood columns and beams running variably down the middle of the space. Initially seen as an impediment to the spatial organization, exhibition layout, and clean mechanical runs, this wiggly line of structure became the generator of all patterns and configurations in the design of the gallery. A luminous ceiling, the office and storage-room walls, and integrated furniture pieces all exist within a pattern system developed from this beam-and-column configuration.

As one of the few available surfaces for design in an art gallery that requires white walls, the ceiling condenses all aspects of the site and program strategies for the gallery in its lighting, organization, and technology. The form of this luminous ceiling volume—constructed of aluminum flat bar, translucent acrylic, and internal and external lighting—makes use of the configuration of the existing structure as it moves through the space across the width of the gallery.

This project was completed in collaboration with Ghislaine Vinas Interior Design.

2

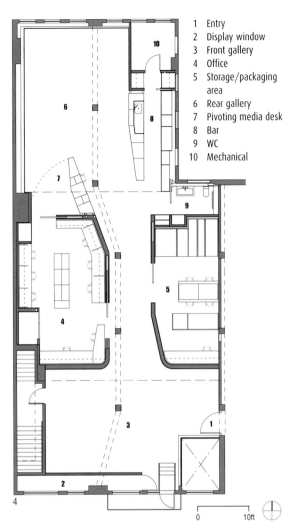

1 Entry
2 Display window
3 Front gallery
4 Office
5 Storage/packaging
area
6 Rear gallery
7 Pivoting media desk
8 Bar
9 WC
10 Mechanical

4

0   10ft

3

1 Front gallery looking towards rear gallery **2** Exterior façade as it faces the street **3** Front gallery
4 Floor plan **5** Rear gallery **Michael Moran**

5

Stockholm Public Library

Stockholm, Sweden

This project is an addition to Erik Gunnar Asplund's 1927 Stockholm Public Library. An international competition invited designs for the expansion of the library, to hold more volumes and departments, while reconsidering the concept of an urban public library at the beginning of the 21st century. When the Stockholm Library was constructed, it gave form to the idea of education and literacy as necessities for Swedish national identity, at once a very local and very national idea. In this design, the library addition is configured around an expanded idea of public place, where local conditions—the existing library, the park, and the city—are reflected in the scheme, but the view is outward in all directions and global.

The existing Stockholm Library organizes books, reading areas, offices, and circulation around a cylindrical rotunda illuminated by clerestory windows. This centralized space and its stripped-down classical language formalized the idea of a literate national populace. For the addition to the iconic building, this luminous central space is reconsidered and transformed into a series of yellow-glass light voids that also carry out heating, cooling, and ventilation. In this regard, the classically centralized void is reborn as an expression of a new idea of public space based on a sustainable and multi-centered organizational system.

1 Aerial site view **2** Roof plan, with skylights for each library department

2

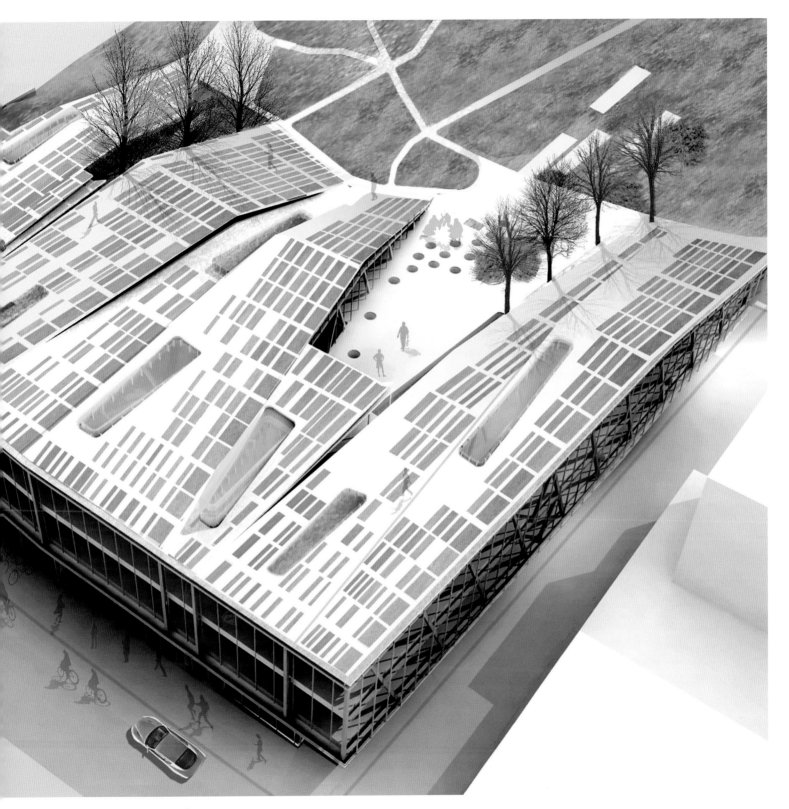

Wetland City
New Orleans East, Louisiana

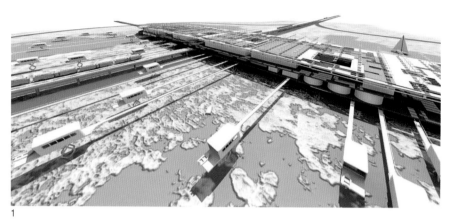

1

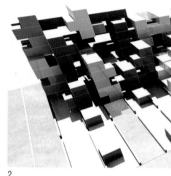

2

In New Orleans post-Hurricane Katrina, high points and high lines were revealed by the rising waters that inundated the lowlands. An understanding of high and low, how to remove water, and where to go during floods is critical to planning a response. Wetland City constructs and protects wetlands, occupies various types of high ground, and builds newly elevated surfaces for sensible habitation. The proposed location for Wetland City, in New Orleans East, was one of the most severely flooded sites during Hurricane Katrina.

Clean, green transit systems, with terminals that double as rescue stations, will be strung along an existing east–west corridor, called Chef Menteur Highway. The neighborhood's existing structure would be extended along the major existing north–south boulevards into a neglected industrial swath of land between Chef Menteur Highway and the Mississippi River Gulf Outlet (MRGO). This area is to be intensely planted to remediate current industrial degradation in the short term (25 to 30 years), and six long land bridges will be

constructed perpendicular to MRGONE Park. New sustainable flood- and storm-resistant neighborhoods would be built, and existing neighborhoods in New Orleans East provided with rescue and community programs and clean public transit systems.

With less land for habitation, Zydeco Urbanism and Zydeco Housing will squeeze the current state of sprawl, much like an accordion, into denser configurations.

The Wetlands International Protection Institute (WIPI) will protect wetlands and build awareness about wetlands issues. It uses the decks of the I-10 highway overpasses as existing high ground, which, by 2050, will hover over water and reestablished wetlands.

A new public transportation system will incorporate a light rail network parallel to bike and pedestrian paths, clean-fuel buses will serve the north–south spines, and transit stations will double as rescue centers.

3

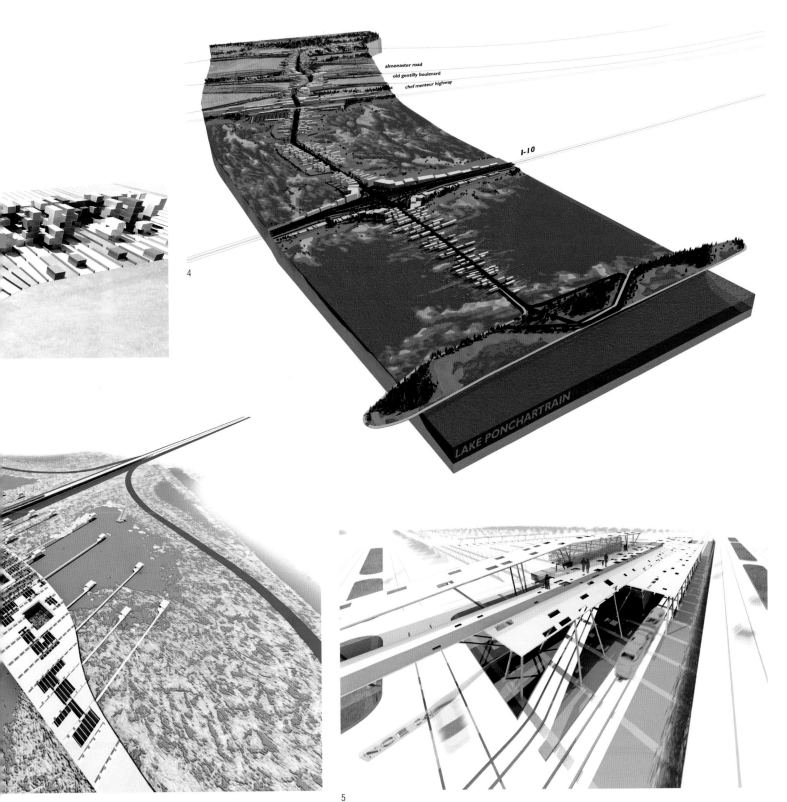

almonaster road
old gentilly boulevard
chef menteur highway

I-10

LAKE PONCHARTRAIN

4

5

Wisdom Exhibition
Sydney, Australia

This exhibition design was for a presentation of photographs, text, and video from a project called Wisdom by Andrew Zuckerman. The work consists of a collection of interviews on the subject of wisdom. The exhibition evolved from a book of the same name. The approach was to take the quotes and photographs and separate them. The text runs around the perimeter of the gallery, while the images are placed in the center, in either a linear or a staggered pattern. This allows the visitor to engage with the text and photos separately as well as together. The text also traveled beyond the gallery and into the lobby and bathrooms.

1 Gallery center, looking across the axis **2** Detail of panel in the gallery center **3** Gallery center, looking down the axis **Andrew Zuckerman**

MOS

25 Mercer Street, Suite 4, New York, New York, 10013

www.mos-office.net

WHO WE ARE:
We are a collective of architects, designers, and thinkers. The two principals, Michael Meredith and Hilary Sample, teach at Harvard University and Yale University, while also running the office. Our office bridges the speculative work of academia with the real-world constraints of practice.

OUR ARCHITECTURAL VALUES IN A DOZEN WORDS:
We value time thinking about architecture and its relevance to contemporary culture.

OUR ARCHITECTURAL PHILOSOPHY IN THREE-DOZEN WORDS:
We believe in rethinking the architectural avant-garde. We're for inclusive practices not exclusive ones. We take pleasure in the mistakes, the pathos, the awkward, the vernacular, the weird, the silly, the frivolous, and the disciplinary minor.

OUR PRACTICE IN 20-DOZEN WORDS:

We don't know exactly when MOS started, but it was sometime in 2003. At first our name was !@#?, which we quickly found too difficult to use because a) you couldn't pronounce it, and b) you couldn't get a web address that included it. Eventually, we drifted towards MOS—an acronym of our names and a shared desire to be horizontal and fuzzy, as opposed to tall and shiny. We began our makeshift office around a large table and began working through a range of design experiments—a make-believe of architectural fantasies, problems, and thoughts about what we would be building if we could only get the work. "MOS definitely" was our slogan.

As we've grown, we have continued to operate around one large table as a small experimental office that works closely on each project through playful experimentation, serious research, and old-fashioned problem solving. Through our work we engage architecture as an open system of interrelated issues ranging from architectural typology, digital methodologies, sustainability, structure, fabrication, materiality, tactility, and use, as well as larger networks of the social, cultural, and environmental. This inclusive process allows MOS to operate, producing and inflecting environments at a multiplicity of scales. We work with a variety of clients all over the world, designing private houses, artist studios, institutional buildings, urban strategies, research, books, installations, furniture, films, and other projects that are less easily categorized. Ultimately, we're a group of collaborators working in perpetuity.

WHY WE PRACTICE IN NEW YORK IN TWO-DOZEN WORDS:

New York is a place that we escape to, because we like to be secluded when working. It plays a crucial role in creativity.

"Afterparty" PS1/MoMA Young Architects Program
Long Island City, New York

According to the *Oxford English Dictionary*, an afterparty is "a party held after another event, especially a concert or another party." The primary purpose of an afterparty is to offer an environment and atmosphere that is different from the earlier venue, typically one that is more relaxed and conducive to socializing.

Today we find ourselves at the afterparty of architecture, rethinking and resituating it. We must consider not only the formal and conceptual economies of architecture, but also its inherent ability to engage and produce visceral and intimate environments. This particular "afterparty" is a temporary urban shelter and passive cooling station for PS1 and its Warm Up events, an escape from the heat in a cooled-down PS1 courtyard.

The project adopts specific structural, material, and organizational logics necessary to produce an evaporative cooling effect by working with the existing airflows of the site (primarily wind from the south to southwest). Cool air generated from the thermal mass of the courtyard's shaded concrete walls and concrete water troughs is drawn up by induction through a series of vent-stack

cooling chimneys, creating a breeze and a "cool down" atmosphere for informal gatherings. The dark thatched skin of the shelter performs similarly to a Bedouin tent.

Here, architecture is honed toward the primitive essentials of space, structure, and environment, where a network of large, medium, and small cellular spaces allow for intimacy and social formations to thrive.

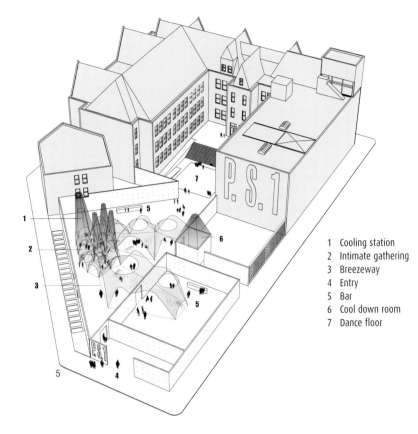

1 Cooling station
2 Intimate gathering
3 Breezeway
4 Entry
5 Bar
6 Cool down room
7 Dance floor

1 Aerial view on opening day **2** Aerial view showing exterior thatch skin **3** Towers from across the street outside the courtyard walls **4** Interior aluminum fabric **5** Axonometric diagram **6** Section
Florian Holzherr

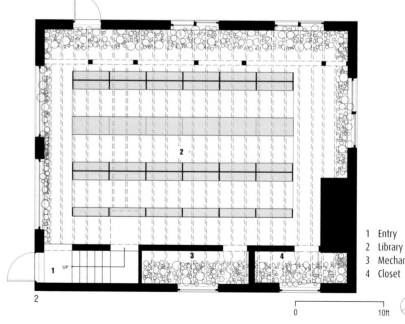

Library and Studio
Princeton, New Jersey

This project involved the renovation of an old barn into a library and studio. The two levels share an economical heating and cooling system, using fans at the top of the ceiling on the second floor to pull the cool air up from the floor below, or to push the warm air down in the winter. The perimeter desk on the second floor works in conjunction with the ventilation panels. All of the existing openings in the façade are glazed with operable windows, and the existing holes in the wood floor were filled with clear resin. The perimeter vents and resin knots allow light and air to pass between the library and the writing studio.

1   Entry
2   Library
3   Mechanical
4   Closet

0   10ft

1 Exterior looking into library interior **2** Floor plan **3** Library interior; bookcases **4** Perimeter light and air vents at night **5** Perimeter vents and continuous desk surface above **6** Milled MDF perimeter vent panel **Michael Vahrenwald**

3

4

5

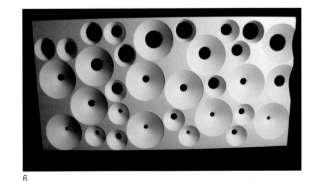

6

Floating House
Lake Huron
Pointe au Baril, Ontario, Canada

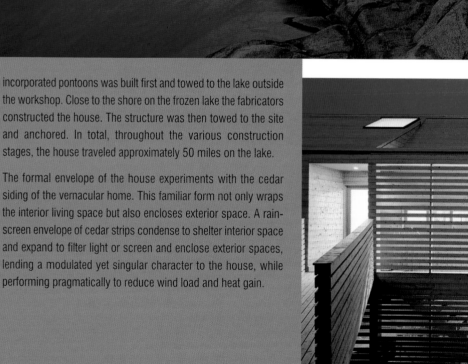

This project intersects a vernacular house typology with the site-specific conditions of a unique setting: an island on Lake Huron. The location of the house imposed complexities on its fabrication and construction, as well as on its relationship to the site. Annual seasonal changes, compounded by escalating global shifts in environmental trends, cause Lake Huron's water levels to vary drastically from month to month and from year to year. To adapt to this constant, dynamic change, the house floats atop a structure of steel pontoons, allowing it to move in synchrony with the water level.

Locating the house on a remote island posed another set of constraints. Using traditional construction processes would have been prohibitively expensive; most of the budget would have been spent transporting building materials to the remote island. Instead, the architect worked with the contractor to devise a prefabrication and construction process that maximized the use of the unique character of the site—its proximity to a waterway. Construction materials were delivered to the contractor's fabrication shop, located on the lake's shore. The steel platform structure with

incorporated pontoons was built first and towed to the lake outside the workshop. Close to the shore on the frozen lake the fabricators constructed the house. The structure was then towed to the site and anchored. In total, throughout the various construction stages, the house traveled approximately 50 miles on the lake.

The formal envelope of the house experiments with the cedar siding of the vernacular home. This familiar form not only wraps the interior living space but also encloses exterior space. A rain-screen envelope of cedar strips condense to shelter interior space and expand to filter light or screen and enclose exterior spaces, lending a modulated yet singular character to the house, while performing pragmatically to reduce wind load and heat gain.

1

2

3

5

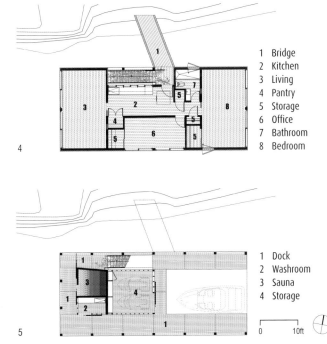

4

1 House and sleeping cabin at dusk 2 Entry elevation showing open wood slats 3 View from living room looking back toward the island 4 Second floor plan 5 First floor plan **Florian Holzherr; MOS**

1 Bridge
2 Kitchen
3 Living
4 Pantry
5 Storage
6 Office
7 Bathroom
8 Bedroom

1 Dock
2 Washroom
3 Sauna
4 Storage

0   10ft

1

Hill House
Honeoye Lake, New York

Hill House is located on Lake Honeoye, in the Finger Lakes region of Upstate New York. The property slopes dramatically toward the water; upon approach the first view of the house is primarily of the roof. The house is located close to the water's edge, nestled in the slope.

The initial design challenge was how to integrate the house into the slope and incorporate the view into the design, while utilizing the lower level to avoid a basement condition. The shape of the roof became a distorted version of the vernacular that reflects and responds to the shape of the site, running parallel and marking plateaus and shifts in the landscape. The interior space is the same shape as the roof. All of the interior spaces open to a large exterior view. The living room offers a panorama of the lake, the bathroom focuses on the sky, and the bedrooms look onto a grove of pear trees. The center of the house is an empty void of exterior space, bringing light and air into the basement and providing a passive ventilation system. At the center, where one might expect to be most removed from the exterior, Hill House becomes transparent and open. The space explodes in a multitude of directions—up, down, forward, backward.

The house expresses the vernacular while also fitting within a reductive modern paradigm—the monochromatic house that is disassociated from its context. Hill House is consciously intertwined with the ground and slope. It is meant to look like a cutout in the landscape, producing a figure-ground effect that switches between object and background.

2

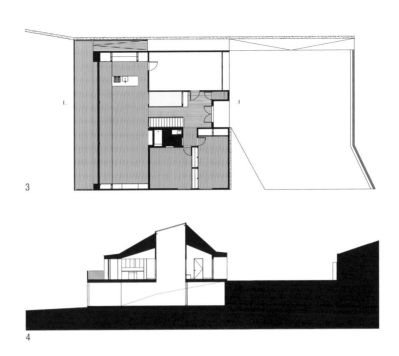

3

4

5

Ordos 100
Ordos, Inner Mongolia

This project draws upon the traditional Chinese courtyard house and nomadic yurt typologies to explore issues of performance and sustainability in the Inner Mongolian desert. This vast and undeveloped site is covered with snow in winter and desert dunes and brush in summer. Throughout the year there are dramatic temperature variations from day to night. Courtyards and thermal chimneys were developed to allow for optimal comfort and natural light. Each living space is designed as a distinct volume, with individual sloping roof forms—all unique to each program.

The organization of the courtyard house is generated through the elimination of hallways. Rooms are connected at their corners, producing localized symmetries. Each spatial activity of the house is divided into separate room types, which are developed as hollow-shell, hip-roofed units. As the unit aggregates, each space takes on a programmatic distinction, reshaping in plan. Utilizing parametric modeling, the more compressed a unit is, the taller it becomes, resulting in six distinct courtyard spaces and 11 rooms, ranging from 4 to 10 meters in height. Working with regional

materials of brick and concrete, each unit is built with structural cast-in-place concrete faced with brick.

All units have a mechanically operated skylight and operable windows on at least two sides. During the summer, air is drawn through the windows at the ground level and exhausted at the top. A majority of the courtyards are filled with lily ponds, establishing an evaporative cool-air mass that cools the entire house. In the winter, with the windows closed and utilizing the mass of the wall, the sun heats the exposed surfaces during the day, reducing the need for mechanical heating. Given the deep porches, courtyards, and skylights, each unit will be washed with indirect light throughout the day.

1 The hollow-shell hip-roofed profiles **2** Model of the overall courtyard house organization **3** Living room and exterior porch at night **4** Ground floor plan MOS

2

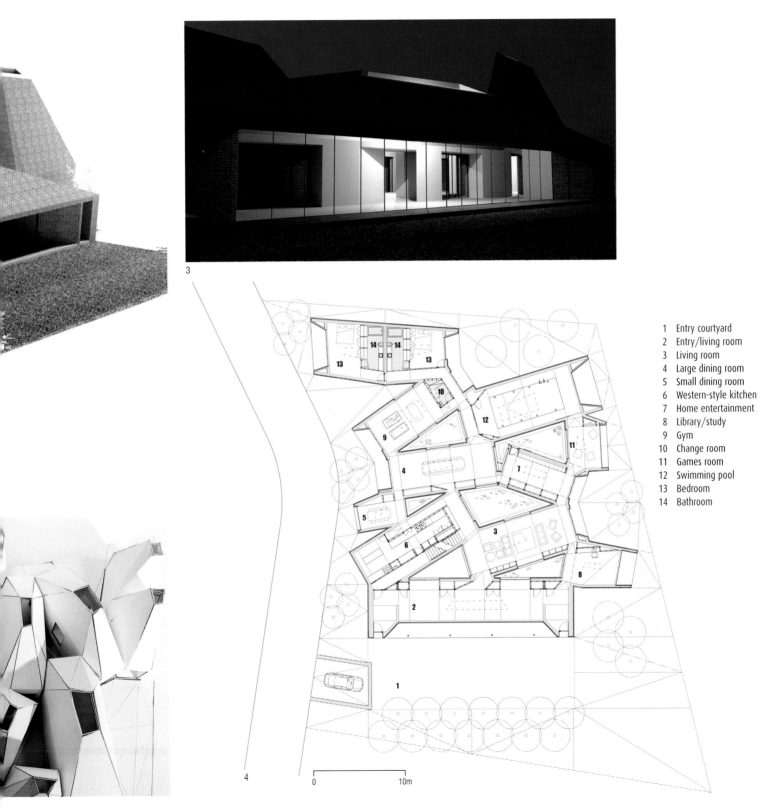

3

4

1   Entry courtyard
2   Entry/living room
3   Living room
4   Large dining room
5   Small dining room
6   Western-style kitchen
7   Home entertainment
8   Library/study
9   Gym
10 Change room
11 Games room
12 Swimming pool
13 Bedroom
14 Bathroom

0   10m

Perforated Metal Storage System
Columbia County, New York

This perforated shed is a continuation of previous research into structural surfaces, and the culmination of a research project to develop a system of flat-packed aluminum panels that arrive onsite, are bent manually, and then bolted together to create a small building. The structure is achieved through folding and overlapping material. The project was designed within a very strict economy of materials and shipping, which involved maximizing the aluminum sheets. The shed is approximately 30 feet long, 6 feet high, and 3 feet deep.

The shed contains garden tools and firewood. The perforations aerate the interior so that the wood remains dry. The perforation patterns were developed through algorithmic scripting to echo the branches of surrounding trees. The result creates a sort of camouflage, where the object starts to visually flatten through transparency and pattern, disintegrating into its environment. The screen wall reflects the surroundings throughout the year. In summer, it takes on hues of green; in winter, the brilliance of a field of snow before it; at dusk it is a backdrop for the shadows of the forest adjacent to it. From the opposite side, shifting light patterns play through the metal panels.

1 Shed exterior with reflections of snow during winter **2** Shed exterior with reflections of foliage during summer **3** Shed from the interior **MOS**

Puppet Theater
Carpenter Center
Cambridge, Massachusetts

1

2

To celebrate the 40th anniversary of Le Corbusier's Carpenter Center, his only building in North America, this theater was constructed within the sunken exterior courtyard for a puppet performance by conceptual artist Pierre Huyghe. The theater's organic form was built with 500 white polycarbonate panels, each one unique. The diamond-shaped panels interlock to become a rigid structure and are simply bolted together so that they can be easily assembled and disassembled.

Once assembled, forces dissipate across the monocoque surface enclosing the theater space. The modulated ceiling panels are turned inside out to accommodate material tolerances, to create skylights, and for structural stability (similar to keystones). The panels are 3 inches deep and span over 15 feet at the center of the theater. Foam inserts in the panels stiffen the plastic shell.

An exterior layer of moss covers the plastic panels. At night, light permeates through the edges of the diagonal panels, causing the moss to appear suspended. Entering into the theater from Quincy Street through a soft, flexible opening designed around a tree, the space bulges to form an interior of reflective, glossy white-plastic walls. Undulating white foam seating repeats the patterning and dimension of the plastic panels, creating a uniform vessel. The interior space compresses, looking toward the stage opening. When not in use, the theater provides a view into the Carpenter Center and upon leaving the soft entrance frames a single tree. The theater collapses the synthetic and organic into a single structural surface.

1 The theater within the sunken courtyard of the Carpenter Center **2** Theater and panels during assembly **3** Interior modulated panels **Florian Holzherr; MOS**

3

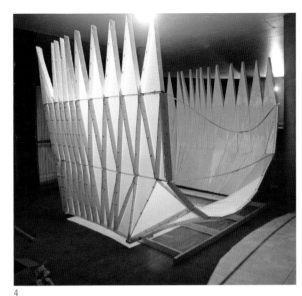

4

5

6

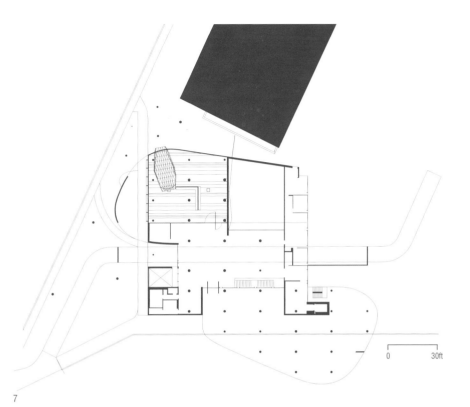

7

0   30ft

8

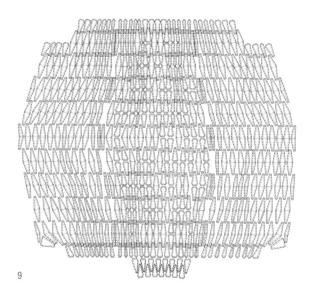

9

4 Theater during assembly **5** Exterior modulated panels with moss inserts **6** Theater entry from Quincy Street **7** Site plan **8** Theater view from underneath the Carpenter Center **9** Diamond-shaped panel patterns **10** View from the interior showing seating **Florian Holzherr; MOS**

10

nARCHITECTS

68 Jay Street, Suite 317, Brooklyn, New York, 11201

www.narchitects.com

WHO WE ARE:
Eric Bunge, AIA & Mimi Hoang, NCARB,
Principals

BRIDGING CONCEPTUAL
THINKING WITH FORMAL
INVENTION.

OUR ARCHITECTURAL VALUES IN A DOZEN WORDS:
Maximum effect with economy of means,
and positive impact on the environment.

OUR ARCHITECTURAL PHILOSOPHY IN THREE-DOZEN WORDS:
We aim to create a body of work that resonates with the needs of
our users and those of culture at large. Design innovation and new
conceptual frameworks are sited within cultural, environmental
and technical contexts.

nARCHITECTS was founded in New York City in 1999 by partners Eric Bunge and Mimi Hoang. In the design of buildings, interiors, ephemeral structures, and public urban spaces we aim for maximum effect with an economy of conceptual and material means and a positive impact on the environment

nARCHITECTS' work has been published in over 15 languages, including the monograph, *DD 29: nARCHITECTS / Eric Bunge & Mimi Hoang, 2000–2008*. Recent awards include AIA Design Honor Awards (2007, 2005), AIA Building Type Merit Award (2008), a NYSCA Award (2007), The Architectural League of New York's Emerging Voices (2006), an AR+D Mention (2006), Architectural Record's Design Vanguard (2004), the MoMA/P.S.1 Young Architects Program (2004), and NYFA grants (Lily Auchincloss Fellows 2008 and 2002), and the 2005 Canadian Professional Rome Prize.

Eric Bunge (born in 1967 Montreal, Canada) received a Masters in Architecture from the Harvard Graduate School of Design in 1996 and a Bachelor of Architecture from McGill University in 1991. He teaches graduate design studios at Columbia University GSAPP, and has taught at Yale University, Harvard University GSD, RISD, and Parsons School of Design.

Mimi Hoang (born in 1971 Saigon, Vietnam) received a Masters in Architecture from Harvard Graduate School of Design in 1998, and a Bachelor of Science in Architecture from M.I.T. in 1993. She teaches graduate design studios at Yale University and Columbia University GSAPP, and has taught at Harvard University GSD and University of California at Berkeley.

FREQUENT COLLABORATORS:
Arup NY
Robert Silman Associates

WHY WE PRACTICE IN NEW YORK IN TWO-DOZEN WORDS:

New York is local and global, walkable and gigantic, anonymous and intimate; a neutral ground that allows outsiders like us to feel like insiders.

1

2

Canopy
Long Island City, New York

Canopy was a temporary structure for the Museum of Modern Art's Young Architects Program, built with green bamboo in the courtyard of P.S.1, a contemporary art and music venue that held weekly Warm Up music parties attracting 8,000 revelers every Saturday in the summer. Museumgoers lounged, played, and danced to some of the most avant-garde DJs and groups visiting New York. The weekday and Sunday audience was quieter, comprising students and families with children. Canopy was host to more than 100,000 visitors during its five months of existence, during which time it underwent a slow transformation as the freshly cut green bamboo turned from green to tan. This rapid transformation emphasized Canopy's brevity, allowing visitors to experience the effects of time in a direct and tactile way.

The architects developed the idea of a "deep landscape" to stitch together the limits of the existing site (ground, concrete walls, sky) with one material. Canopy relied on a singular tectonic system for shade, structure, and atmosphere. Pinches in the undulating lattice produced a range of shadow densities and patterns across the courtyard. Dips in the canopy defined rooms that were open to the sky, each with a distinct climatic environment for different modes of lounging: Pool Pad incorporated a large wading pool; Fog Pad was surrounded by nozzles that spread a halo of cool mist on revelers; Rainforest featured a sound environment and misters that provided intermittent rain showers and randomly soaked the crowd; and Sand Hump's sandy cove maximized exposure to either sun or shade.

142

3

4

5

1 The weekly Warm Up music parties attracted up to 8,000 people every Saturday in the summer
2 Canopy relied on a singular tectonic system for shade, structure, and atmosphere **3** Canopy was host to more than 100,000 visitors throughout its five months of existence **4** The architects and their team of students and recent graduates spent six weeks on site testing each arc type to determine the maximum span, minimum bending radii, and overlap dimensions, before building the structure itself over a period of seven weeks **5** The project utilized 9,400 meters of flexible, freshly cut green *Philostachys aurea* bamboo from Georgia, spliced and bound together with 11,300 meters of stainless-steel wire **Sam DuFaux; nARCHITECTS; Frank Oudeman**

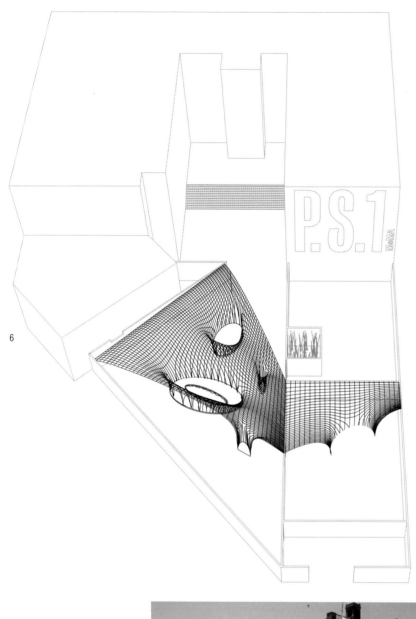

6

7

8

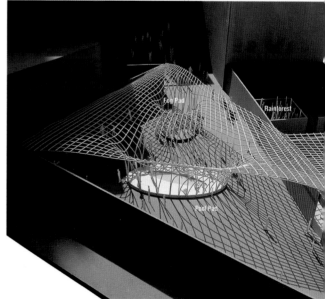

9

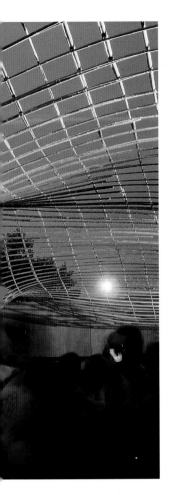

10

6 Axonometric **7** Dips in the canopy provoke different modes of lounging in four distinct environments **8** Each arc was assembled on the ground by splicing together 7-meter bamboo poles with stainless-steel wire and marking off each intersection point **9** Pinches in the canopy produce a range of shadow densities **10** Pool Pad incorporated a large wading pool **Sam DuFaux; nARCHITECTS; Frank Oudeman; Jorge Periera**

Dune Terrace: Grand Egyptian Museum
Giza, Egypt

1,2 The permanent gallery level is housed in a floating bar, clad in a light-filtering perforated concrete envelope **3** Visitors arrive on the Dune Terrace, a spectacular shaded exterior viewing platform situated slightly above the level of the plateau
nARCHITECTS

1

As a critique of the museum as a reified curatorial circuit, the architect's proposal (with Ove Arup & Partners, NY) envisions additional modes of navigation based on airport organizational models. Visitors to the new 860,000-square-foot museum of perforated concrete, steel, glass, and stone arrive by bus onto the Dune Terrace, a spectacular 1,000-foot exterior viewing platform that frames the pyramids beyond.

Five lobbies/galleries lead to the permanent collections in a floating bar above, and to the temporary gallery, convention center, and sculpture gardens below. In the spirit of a campus plan, these lobbies/galleries offer visitors various ways of experiencing the museum: traditional gallery circuit, easy overviews, random surfing, and rapid access to specific galleries. In the floating bar of galleries above, the collection is organized chronologically in east–west thematic bands. A series of north–south concourses allow for physical and virtual crossovers into other galleries or virtual sites.

2

4

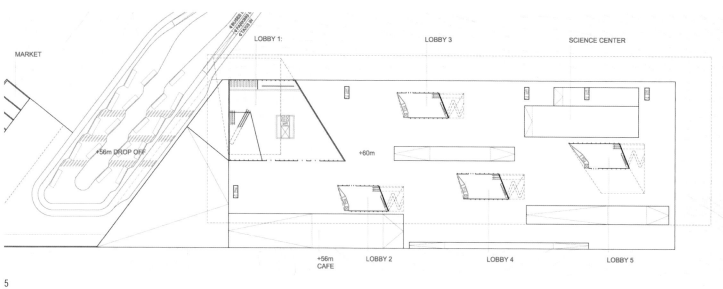

5

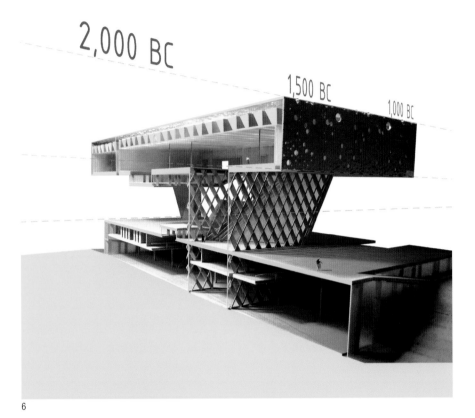

2,000 BC

1,500 BC

1,000 BC

4 Five lobbies allow for alternate circuits: easy overview, random surfing, and rapid access to specific galleries **5** Entry level plan **6** At the gallery level, the collection is organized chronologically from west to east. While the majority of visitors will move forward in time in this direction, along five thematic routes, their entry point will depend on which lobby they have arrived from. **7** In the spirit of airport departure gates, visitors can choose from five lobbies, depending on which part of the collection above they wish to visit, or which program below they need to access **8** Upper galleries plan **nARCHITECTS**

6

7

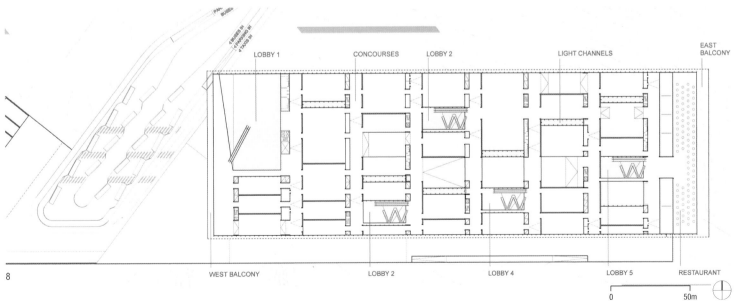

LOBBY 1   CONCOURSES   LOBBY 2   LIGHT CHANNELS   EAST BALCONY

8   WEST BALCONY   LOBBY 2   LOBBY 4   LOBBY 5   RESTAURANT

0   50m

1 Curatorial plan **2** An endless table meanders through The Drawing Center's Gallery **3** The table displayed 70 of Frederick Kiesler's drawings and one of his notebooks **4** The endless table is fabricated with powder-coated CNC-milled aluminum, acrylic, and MDF **5** Along the way, visitors face each other from varying distances across an inaccessible void in the center of the gallery **6** Details: the angles of the display vary according to size, causing visitors to adjust their viewpoints
Frank Oudeman

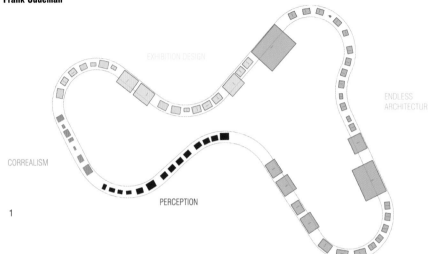

EXHIBITION DESIGN

ENDLESS
ARCHITECTURE

CORREALISM

PERCEPTION

1

2

3

Kiesler Exhibition: Endless Table
New York, New York

A 145-foot-long (yet seemingly endless) table meanders through The Drawing Center's Gallery in a single loop, displaying 70 of Frederick Kiesler's drawings and one notebook. The walls of the gallery are left blank for the first time in The Drawing Center's history. Visitors are guided along a curatorial itinerary divided into four themes relevant to the avant-garde architect's work: Correalism, Perception, Endless Architecture, and Exhibition Design. Along the way, visitors face each other from varying distances across an inaccessible void in the center of the gallery. Larger drawings are displayed on tilted panels, generating surprise and causing visitors to adjust their viewpoints. Endless Table was fabricated with powder-coated CNC-milled aluminum, acrylic, and MDF, and was assembled in two days. The V-shaped aluminum table legs are designed to both support the table and structurally join together its 21 reconfigurable modules.

The exhibition explores the pivotal role drawing played in the interdisciplinary and multifaceted work of Austro-American designer, artist, theoretician, and architect, Frederick Kiesler (1890–1965). *Frederick Kiesler: Co-Realities* traces Kiesler's interest in the expressive and conceptual possibilities of drawing through key projects and concepts from the 1930s to the 1960s, from his early work as a scenic designer to his revolutionary designs for Peggy Guggenheim's Art of the Century Gallery, and his decades-long investigation into the unique structure of his Endless House. As so few of Kiesler's installations, sets, or projects remain or were ever realized, the drawings have become key to understanding his significant contribution to 20th-century thought.

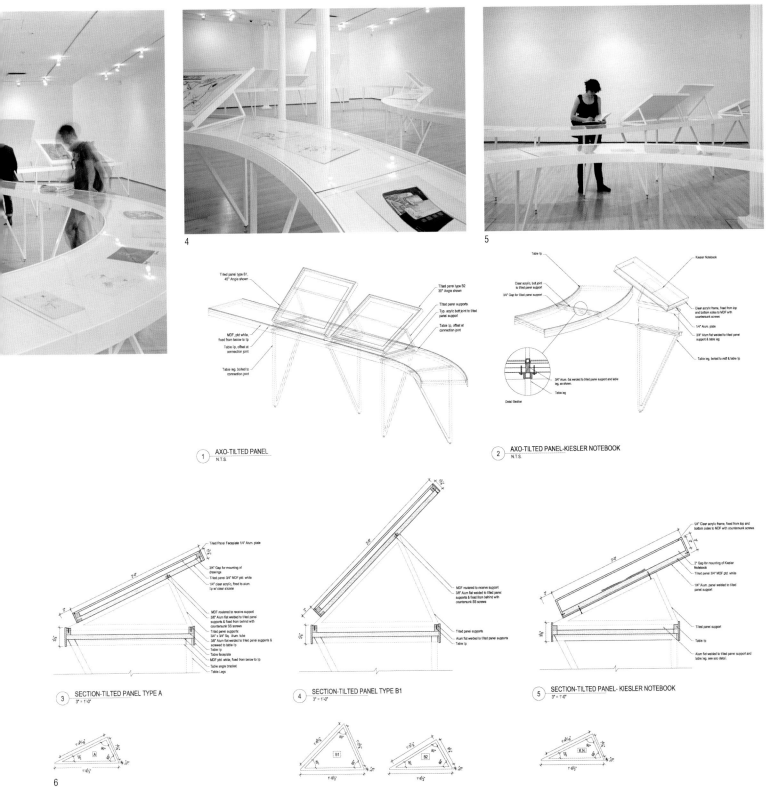

4

5

1. AXO-TILTED PANEL
N.T.S.

2. AXO-TILTED PANEL-KIESLER NOTEBOOK
N.T.S.

3. SECTION-TILTED PANEL TYPE A
3" = 1'-0"

4. SECTION-TILTED PANEL TYPE B1
3" = 1'-0"

5. SECTION-TILTED PANEL- KIESLER NOTEBOOK
3" = 1'-0"

6

1

Living Steel
Wuhan, China

As part of the competition brief to promote the use of steel in a low- to middle-income sustainable housing prototype, this project develops the notion of "Living Steel" in three ways that respond to Wuhan's sub-tropical climate and unique demographics.

Residents live within cross-ventilated spaces bounded by living, breathing steel layers, or Living Screens. Vines supported by stainless steel cables on the south façade screen exterior "streets"; a punctured wall of colorful prefabricated steel modules contains infrastructure, distributes captured rainwater, and limits heat gain; and on the north façade a veil of permeable steel balconies is angled to bounce eastern light.

A progression of three typologies emerges like a tree root from the ground, from narrow townhouses below, to wide apartments above. Typical discrepancies in desirability of apartments are minimized: lower and narrower units are compensated with higher ceiling heights, while wider apartments have lower ceiling heights yet better views on higher floors. In this way, the flexible steel framework allows for changing demographics and a variety of lifestyles.

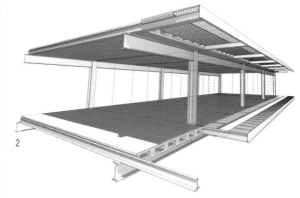

2

The expressive potential of steel construction allows for the soaring cantilevers of three distinct vertical Living Neighborhoods, each defined by one of three apartment types. This shifting of the building mass-produces unique public exterior spaces, each with a different orientation and altitude to be enjoyed at different times of the day.

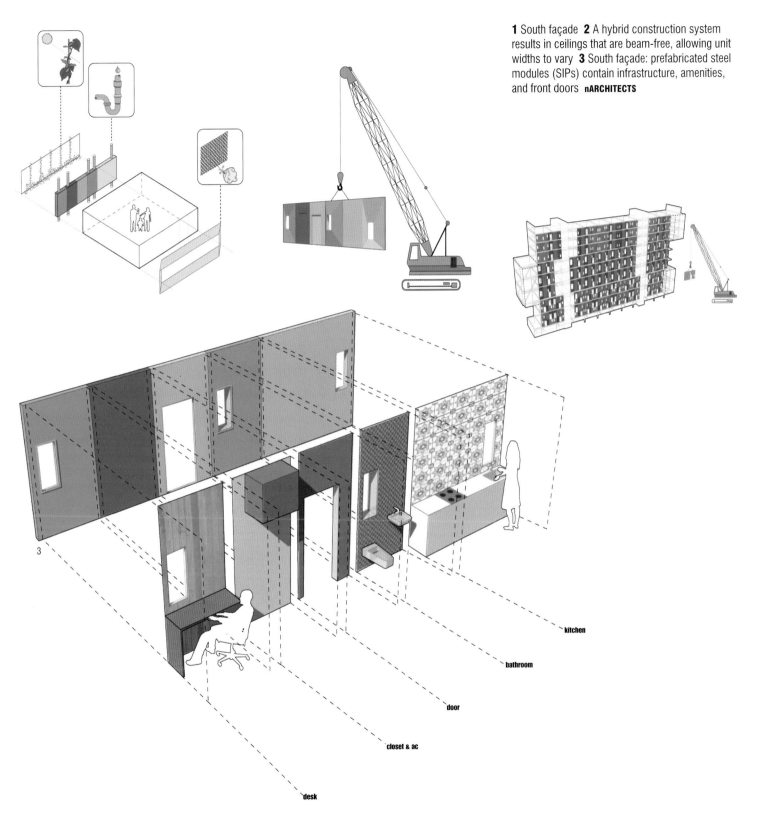

1 South façade **2** A hybrid construction system results in ceilings that are beam-free, allowing unit widths to vary **3** South façade: prefabricated steel modules (SIPs) contain infrastructure, amenities, and front doors **nARCHITECTS**

3

kitchen

bathroom

door

closet & ac

desk

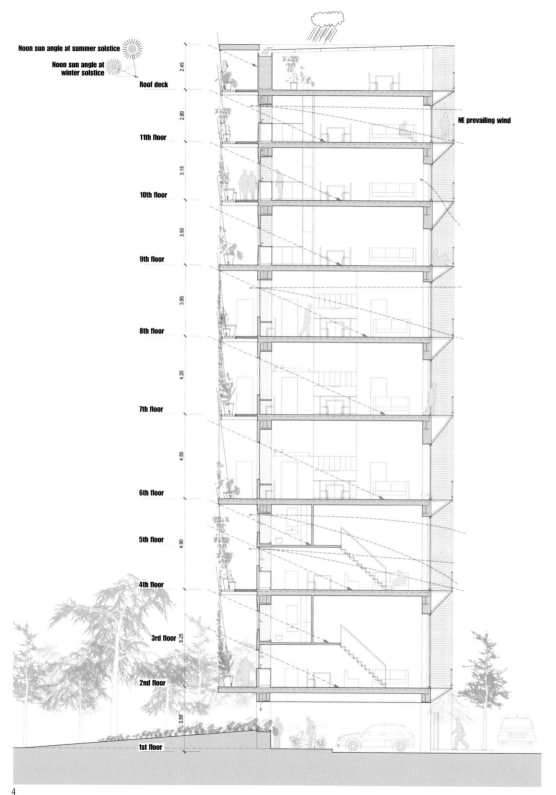

Noon sun angle at summer solstice
Noon sun angle at winter solstice

Roof deck

2.45

11th floor

2.80

10th floor

3.15

9th floor

3.50

8th floor

3.85

7th floor

4.20

6th floor

4.55

5th floor

4.90

4th floor

3rd floor

5.25

2nd floor

3.50

1st floor

NE prevailing wind

4

5

6

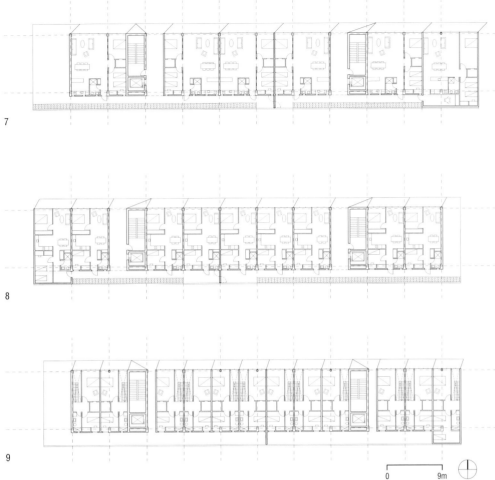

7

8

9

0   9m

4 The project optimizes the use of space with three distinct climatic zones. A compact volume of conditioned interior spaces is enveloped by protective exterior zones: public "streets," shared terraces, private balconies, and a corrugated galvanized metal roof/sunshade that both collects rainwater and shades the top slab, avoiding heat gain. **5** North façade: perforated steel balconies angled to optimize eastern light and prevailing northeast wind **6** South façade **7** Floors 9, 10, 11: the 9-meter-wide lofts **8** Floors 6, 7, 8: the 6-meter-wide lofts **9** Floors 2–5: 4.5-meter-wide double-height units **nARCHITECTS**

1 Bay windows at the front façade switch back and forth allowing views up and down Norfolk Street 2 The residential lobby is designed as a wooden tube 3 The penthouse apartment connects various spaces to a large roof terrace 4 Lobby and gallery floor plan **nARCHITECTS; Frank Oudeman**

Switch Building
New York, New York

Switch Building is a seven-story apartment building and art gallery at 109 Norfolk Street on the Lower East Side. The building consists of four floor-through apartments, a duplex penthouse, and a double-height art gallery on the ground and cellar levels.

The project's design emerges from a creative interpretation of some of the narrow constraints imposed by zoning and the developer's needs. The "switching" concept opportunistically maximizes difference while maintaining the efficiencies of repetition. In a reinterpretation of a traditional New York bay window, an angled front façade switches back and forth, allowing each floor-through apartment unique views up and down Norfolk Street and creating subtle variations in shadows and reflections. From the inside, the bay windows provide deep window seats surrounded by warm hardwood.

At the rear of each apartment, the living space extends out to large balconies—the largest allowed by zoning—which also shift side to side, creating double-height spaces between balconies to maximize afternoon light and neighborly interactions. While the apartment plans are identical, these variations allow each unit to be unique in its light qualities and views to the city.

The new nonprofit Switch Gallery expands its boundaries with the street via a black hot-rolled steel and glass storefront and canopy that open completely to the sidewalk. At the rear of the gallery, visitors descend into a double-height volume illuminated by a large skylight. The gallery's plan maximizes wall space in a fluid spatial continuity, while working around the obstacles of the residential core and lobby with which it shares its footprint. The gallery introduces a larger scale into the Lower East Side's burgeoning art scene, which has been primarily inserting cultural programs into former tenement buildings.

2

3

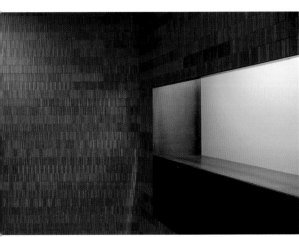

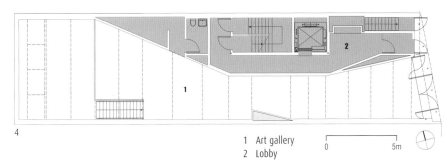

4

1 Art gallery
2 Lobby

0   5m

5

6

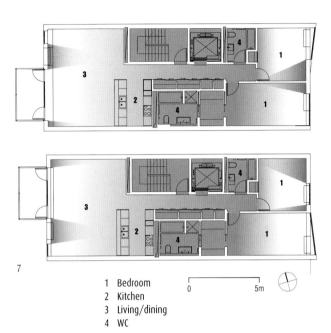

1 Bedroom
2 Kitchen
3 Living/dining
4 WC

0   5m

7

5 At the rear of the gallery, visitors descend into a double-height volume illuminated by a large skylight **6** The bathroom of the penthouse apartment **7** Plans of typical apartments **nARCHITECTS; Frank Oudeman**

Windshape
Lacoste, France

1 Windshape became a central public meeting space throughout the summer of 2006 **2** The local winds and the Mistral gave shape to constantly mutating structures **3** The pavilions were illuminated at night against the backdrop of the Marquis de Sade's castle, and were visible from as far away as the village of Bonnieux, 5 kilometers away **4** Windshape refers in its exterior form and angular geometry to the medieval townscape of Lacoste **5** By varying the degree of tension in the string, the architects built Windshape to respond to the wind in several ways, from rhythmic oscillations to fast ripples across its surface **nARCHITECTS; Daniela Zimmer**

2

1

Windshape was an ephemeral structure commissioned by the Savannah College of Art & Design (SCAD) as a venue and gathering space near their Provence campus in Lacoste, France. Built by the architects and a team of SCAD students over a period of five weeks, Windshape became the small town's main public meeting space, and hosted concerts, exhibitions, and ceremonies throughout the summer of 2006.

Windshape was conceived as two 8-meter-high pavilions that dynamically change with the Provençal wind. A vine-like structural network of white plastic pipes, joined together and stretched apart by aluminum collars, emerged from the limestone walls and terraces of Lacoste's hillside. Approximately 50 kilometers of white polypropylene string was threaded through the lattice to create swaying enclosures. The string was woven into dense

regions and surfaces and pinched to define doorways, windows, and spaces for seating.

By varying the degree of tension in the string, the architects built Windshape to respond to the wind in several ways, from rhythmic oscillations to fast ripples across its surfaces. During heavy winds, Windshape moved dramatically, and made a hissing sound akin to dozens of jump ropes. The pavilions took on a multitude of temporary forms over the course of the summer, as they billowed in and out, and momentarily came to rest.

Windshape was a laboratory for testing the idea of a building that can respond to natural stimuli. Rather than simply sheltering people from the elements, buildings of the future could also connect inhabitants to their environment, reminding them of its strength and beauty.

3

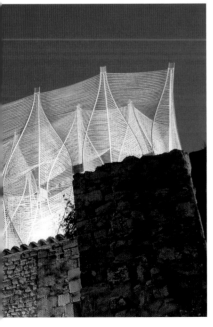

4

5

studio S U M O

44-02 23rd Street, #209, Long Island City, New York, 11101
3-26 Kioi-cho, Chiyoda-ku, Tokyo

www.studiosumo.com

CONTEXT
[OBJECTS+SUBJECTS+CIRCUITS]
UTILITY+PLEASURE

WHO WE ARE:
Yolande Daniels, Sunil Bald, Anees Assali, Eddie Yujoong Kim, David Huang, Shai Turner, Nathan King, Laura Lee

OUR ARCHITECTURAL VALUES IN A DOZEN WORDS:
Architectural complexity is derived from interplays between material mediation and contextual meditation.

OUR ARCHITECTURAL PHILOSOPHY IN THREE-DOZEN WORDS:
Architecture arises in the spatial translation of events. SUMO approaches each project anew by incorporating meaningful play to reframe assumptions about utility and allow the transformation of abstract reflections into the production of objects and space.

studio S U M O formulates architectural complexity in work generated from a layered reading of context, materials, objects, and spatial production. This development bridges the decades when architects found new points of engagement in the identification of diverse subjects and explored innovations in methods of fabrication and architectural production as a global cultural commodity. Our work draws from each of these discourses to reframe contexts as shifting between social constructions, cultural conditions, and physical environments. Our interest in the interplay between architectural and social constructions is understood in the interweaving of objects, subjects, and circuits.

In domestic projects, we consider context as both inward and outward, where private desires and aspirations are addressed through economies of scale. In institutional projects—especially installations, exhibitions, and museum designs—our interest is in the dynamic relationship between social and architectural narratives as the embodiment of the dynamic between rhetorical and physical constructions. The historical and cultural context is the generator of architectural invention. In projects that integrate architectural and urban concerns we have developed strategies for the mutual inflection of circuits and architecture. These projects have allowed us to explore the interplay between flows and objects as social generators and spatial keys at a variety of scales.

This dynamic conception of context that is embedded in objects, reflected in subjects, and networked in circuits—and which engages body, culture, and community—continues to evolve with the scope, scale, and diversity of our work.

WHY WE PRACTICE IN NEW YORK IN TWO-DOZEN WORDS:

Our practice is situated in the margins, in Queens (the most diverse borough in New York), and extends from the United States to Japan.

FREQUENT COLLABORATORS:

Obayashi Corporation, Tokyo Japan: Assoc. Architects/Construction Company
Gilsanz, Murray, Steficek, New York: Engineers
Ove Arup, New York: Engineers
Buro Happold, New York: Engineers
David Huang: Videos, renderings
Anees Assali: Web design, renderings

Harlem Duplex
Harlem, New York, New York

1 Existing townhouse (this project is on the top two floors) **2** Dining nook **3** View of kitchen console towards stair **4** Steel stair **5** Section
Frank Oudeman

This 1,200-square-foot apartment interior and roof deck renovation was commissioned by a young British bachelor who chose to make Harlem his home. The aspiration was to create a minimal and monastic retreat in the heart of Harlem from a heavily compartmentalized 16-foot-wide space. Walls and ceilings were removed and domestic programs (including kitchen, entertainment consoles, closets, and toilets) are incorporated in linear strips along the party walls. These ribbons transform rooms into consoles: entertainment surfaces, an appliance tower, and toilet and dressing bars, among others. Newly added windows and skylights accentuate the vistas through and out of the apartment, taking advantage of the openness produced by this "console" approach to program.

A cantilevered steel stair and bridge were inserted into a cut spanning the width of the apartment. This light structure couples with a new façade to the roof deck at the rear, bringing light into the center of the apartment. A high-gloss ceiling bounces light onto the glass ribbons that reflect into the space.

The stair leads to the bedroom loft and the roof deck on the other side of the steel bridge. The tall folded ceiling surface reveals the steep dormer of the building and is flanked by two consoles, one holding a toilet and sink, the other a closet. These consoles also hold a rack for the owner's sneaker collection, and an open shower with glass held off by a pipe that also serves as the showerhead. The 500-square-foot wood deck with flush skylights is beyond, providing a horizon for the tall, compact bed/shower loft. When privacy is required, the space can be closed off with a series of pocketing door panels.

1

2

3

4

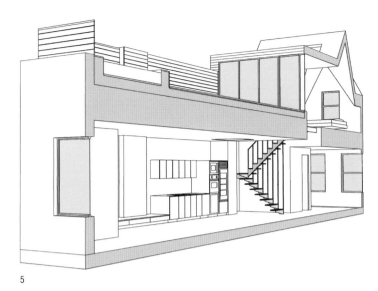

5

7

8

6 View to sleeping nook
7 Sleeping nook flanked by sneaker display **8** Bedroom shower opened to roof deck
Frank Oudeman

Josai School of Management

Sakado, Japan

1

2

The Josai School of Management is located on the Josai University campus, about 45 minutes north of Tokyo. The 70,000-square-foot cast-in-place concrete building contains classrooms, faculty offices, a graduate student center, two auditoria with seating capacities of 250 and 400, presentation classrooms, seminar rooms, a media lab providing computer services for students, and a café. In addition, the project provides lounges and informal meeting areas for students.

The site rises 2 meters on its south end and 9 meters further on its west end to an under-utilized path that runs along the hillside. The building, which responds to this oddly contoured and multi-level site in both plan and section, can be considered a single loaded bar that turns back onto itself and connects head-to-tail through a glass bridge. This divides the site into three distinct landscape zones. Additionally, the sloping floors of the auditoria negotiate the varying site levels to create a dynamic path that slips under the building to an internal courtyard and the hillside beyond. This path is bracketed by informal and accessible public spaces.

The sloped floors of the auditoria help bridge the site levels to intertwine building and path. Classroom blocks served by light-filled circulation zones occupy the upper three floors and project a secondary façade of color, pattern, and graphics. Moving under the bridging slab, one passes the media lab, a wireless space for working alone or collaboratively, to a set of stairs leading to the second-level courtyard, a social core formed by the void of the winding slab. This outdoor room is bracketed by the main stair to the east, the glass bridge to the west, and the classrooms to the north and south. The courtyard is punctured by elliptical skylights that illuminate the media lab below, where custom-designed seating for group gatherings follows the contours of the skylights.

A glass façade with intermittent operable windows allows both light and fresh air to flow through this zone, creating an unbroken and continuous circuit of air and movement. Cooler air from the expansive north façade and the shaded, internal courtyard mixes with the warmer air that collects along the more compressed south façade, greatly reducing conditioning requirements.

3

5

6

4

1 Overall view from northeast **2** Interior media room **3** View from south showing small auditorium with class block above **4** View of inner court to main stair **5** View from north showing large auditorium with class block above **6** View of inner court to glass bridge **Kudoh Photo, Ltd.; Nacasa Photo Ltd.**

1 Aerial view of MINiMAX
2 Exterior view 3 After being delivered by truck, the house is sited and expanded 4 The components of the house and service systems 5 Exterior view along the extended elevation

1

2

MINiMAX is a pre-fabricated, 1,500-square-foot home based on modularity and mass-production at two scales: the shell and the interior components. MINiMAX arrives at the site compressed as a self-contained and structured six-sided mass-produced shell, 15.5 feet wide by 54.5 feet long, containing a flexible domestic interior. Once secured on the site, the end panels fold down as floor extensions and the exterior stairs increasing the overall length to 85 feet. The two end sections of the container slide out along the floor-beds on motorized tracks. These extensions form the living area and master bedroom. The center section is slid laterally to form a second bedroom, opening up the center of the house. The ensuing void is then planted to form an internal garden, which is flanked by entertainment and exercise activities that can extend outdoors.

The MINiMAX structure and exterior enclosure is formed by an exterior shell and a flexible bellows. The bellows is made of an electrically circuited coated mesh and is a source of energy distribution for the interior and components.

Within MINiMAX, zones are defined by an alterable collection of program components. Each component is a self-contained and structured two-sided mass-produced unit 8.5 feet wide by 8.5 feet high by 3 feet deep. The components are optional units that unfold to reveal lifestyle features: from entertainment consoles and exercise equipment to home office systems. They arrive pre-selected and secured to a floor track set into the floor-bed. After the shell sections are extended, the components are unlocked and slid along motorized tracks. Each component can be slid back to open up the spatial core for another activity.

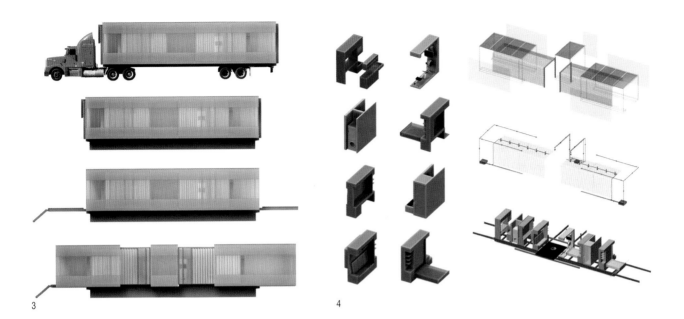

3

4

5

6 Interior view of gym and projection component **7** Interior view of living component **8** Interior view of kitchen component

7

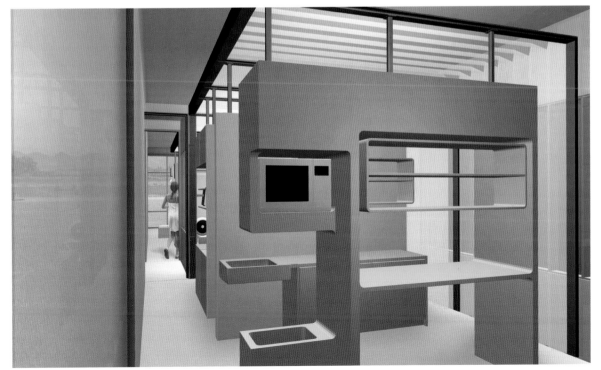

8

Mizuta Museum of Art
Saitama, Japan

This 6,200-square-foot university museum is designed for simultaneous gallery displays. It is essentially two museums that sit side by side. The museum will exhibit, on a rotating basis, pieces from an important collection of 18th- and 19th-century woodcuts in a long, light-controlled area. It will also provide galleries illuminated by slits of north light for temporary university and traveling exhibitions. A continual flow between these two types of exhibition is facilitated through a simple gridding of a warehouse-type space.

The site is between a small road and a newly developing pharmacy complex surrounding a small agricultural area. The museum adds a third edge to this garden, making a pastoral courtyard and circulation route to the pharmacy school. The relatively long and narrow site is preceded by a smaller courtyard that forms an entry to the museum and separates it from a mechanical yard surrounded by trees. This vertical green is brought up to the entry façade of the museum. The museum can be considered a sloped shed that ramps up to two gallery levels and down to a glass-enclosed gathering area sunk 2 meters below existing grade. The

sloping eliminates the need for a freight elevator. The interior gallery walls are trusses that cantilever over a retaining wall, and are tied back into the ground. This allows for the gathering space to be column-free, with the hovering structure of the museum forming its shelter.

The slits in the façade perform in multiple ways. At the ramped entry walkway, the openings are glazed for intermittent views of visitors moving up into the building. The ramps on both sides also form an environmental buffer for the galleries. As the wall turns to the north-facing sloped roof, the openings are glazed with translucent material to allow filtered north light into the temporary gallery space. As the roof passes over the woodcut galleries, the slits ventilate roof-mounted mechanical-equipment between the skin and the gallery space. Finally, as the surface turns to form the east wall, the slits remain open, creating a ventilated, shaded area with an active play of light and shadow around the ramp that slopes to the sunken gathering area. The museum is scheduled to open at the end of 2011.

5

1 Entry view: north face **2** View of south face: gallery above and event space below
3 Light gallery **4** Ramp down to event space **5** Ramp up to gallery **6** Sectional diagram
showing structural truss walls **7** View from event space

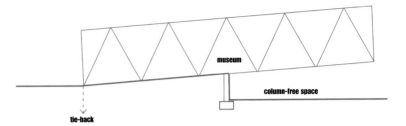

museum

column-free space

tie-back

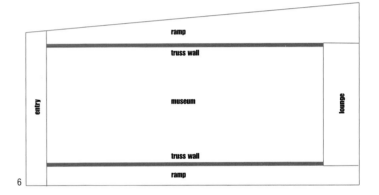

ramp

truss wall

entry

museum

lounge

truss wall

ramp

6

7

MoCADA
Brooklyn, New York

MoCADA, the Museum of Contemporary African Diasporan Art, is the first public art institution to open in the new BAM Cultural District, the Brooklyn project master planned by Rem Koolhaas and Diller/Scofidio around the Brooklyn Academy of Music. This 1,800-square-foot museum is sited in an historic neighborhood on the ground floor of 80 Arts, a center for art organizations, which is housed in a renovated office building. Spotlighting contemporary work of African-American and Caribbean artists, the project weaves together the interests of the existing community and the future arts complex.

While compact, the space has a street presence, and the fenestration of the original office building is being utilized to project the museum's institutional identity. Long and narrow, a reception area open to the corner leads to a gallery that can be reconfigured through a series of pivoting walls. The gallery is illuminated by a floating plane of plastic tubes encased in fiberglass to provide an even, diffuse light while screening the mechanical system. A map at the museum entrance shows the global presence of the African diaspora, and this is expanded upon inside with the entire reception area representing a map.

The reception area is divided evenly into the world's 24 time zones, demarcated with more than 2,000 pieces of wood, stacked in an offset manner, to make an environmental map that locates key cities in the migration of people of African descent. While the reception construction operates as a literal map, it contorts three-dimensionally to address the various programmatic needs of the reception area. On one wall, pockets hold catalogs and other items for sale. Another surface folds to form the desk and transaction counter. This, in turn, connects to a freestanding screen that provides privacy for a small office for museum personnel.

1 Exterior view from corner **2** Reception area/lobby store **3** View to street from lobby store **4** View to street along diaspora wall **5** Diaspora wall **Frank Oudeman**

2

3

4

5

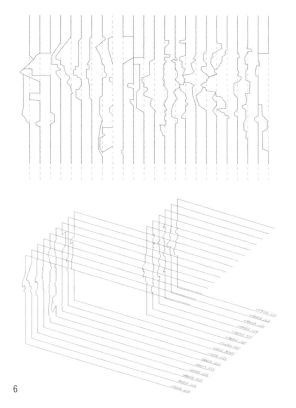

6

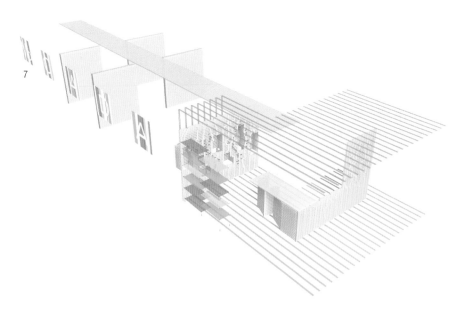

7

6 Spatial mapping of world's time zones **7** Project components **8** Translation of time zones into reception area **9** Diaspora display wall detail **10** Gallery with pivoting walls **Frank Oudeman**

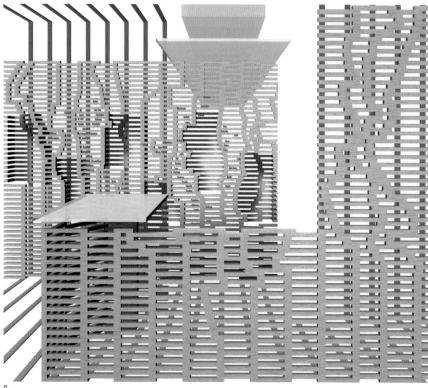

8

MONTREAL
TORONTO
CHICAGO   DETROIT   NEW YORK   BROOKLYN
                        PHILADELPHIA
          ST LOUIS
          WASHINGTON DC
          BIRMINGHAM
                        CHARLESTON
OUSTON
                        JACKSONVILLE
    MEXICO CITY   MIAMI
    PORT AU PRINCE   HAVANNA   NASSAU
                KINGSTON   SANTO DOMINGO
            ARUBA   SAN JUAN
    PANAMA CITY   MARTINIQUE
        BOGOTA
                    CARACAS

9

156 Ludlow Street, 3rd Floor, New York, New York, 10002

WORK Architecture Company (WORKac)

www.work.ac

WHO WE ARE:
Amale Andraos, Dan Wood

OUR ARCHITECTURAL VALUES IN A DOZEN WORDS:
First, do no harm; Second, do nothing banal; Third, do do something

OUR ARCHITECTURAL PHILOSOPHY IN THREE-DOZEN WORDS:
WORKac strives to develop architectural and urban planning projects that engage culture and consciousness, nature and artificiality, surrealism, and pragmatism. We are continually searching in our work for the perfect meeting point between idea and form.

OUR PRACTICE IN 20-DOZEN WORDS:

WORKac is involved in projects at all scales, ranging from a master plan for the new BAM cultural district in Brooklyn, to a single-family villa in Inner Mongolia. Recent completed projects include the installation "Public Farm 1" at P.S.1/MoMA and the new headquarters for Diane von Furstenberg. Current work includes the new Kew Gardens Hills Library in Queens, the extension of the Clark Art Institute at Mass MoCA, a new Children's Museum for the Arts, and the first Edible Schoolyard New York City with Alice Waters' Chez Panisse Foundation. In addition, WORKac's entry for the redesign of Hua Qiang Bei Road, Shenzhen, was recently awarded first place in an international competition.

The practice has international roots; the partners have lived and worked in Europe, the Middle East, and Asia, and WORKac's staff is drawn from different cultures and countries. Difference is harnessed as inspiration.

In 2009, WORKac was a finalist in the National Design Awards. In 2008, the firm was identified by *Icon Magazine* as one of the 25 most influential new architecture firms in the world, and won numerous awards, including several AIA Merit Awards, three "Best of" awards, and a MASterwork Award from the Municipal Arts Society.

The practice is supplemented by the partners' academic involvement. Together they teach at Princeton University, focusing on the relationship between ecology and urbanism. This research is the subject of their book *49 Cities*, published in 2009 by the Storefront for Art and Architecture.

WHY WE PRACTICE IN NEW YORK IN TWO-DOZEN WORDS:

We wonder why sometimes. NYC can be very small for somewhere so big. Then something clicks and we remember: NYC can also be exhilarating.

FREQUENT COLLABORATORS:

Prem Krishnamurthy and Adam Michaels, Graphic Designers, Project Projects
Dan Sesil, Structural Engineer, LERA
Elodie Blanchard, Artist, ElasticCo
Suzan Tillotson, Lighting Designer, Tillotson Design Associates
Feng Guochuan, Architect, Shenzhen Zhubo Design and Consulting Company
Diana Balmori, Landscape Architect, Balmori Associates
Mouna Andraos, Designer, Electronic Crafts
Raymond Quinn, Mechanical Engineer, ARUP
David Taylor, Theatre Consultant, ARUP
Carlos Burbano, Expeditor and Code Consultant, CCBS

Anthropologie Dos Lagos

Corona, California

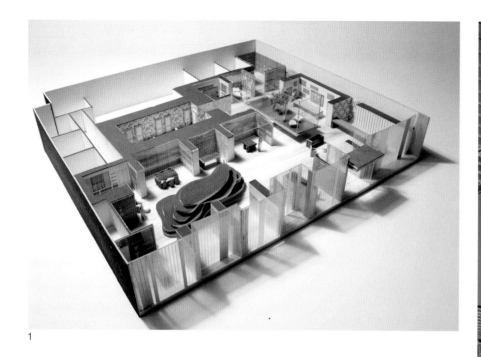

1

1 Model shot **2** View of interior courtyard **following pages** View of main façade **Elizabeth Felicella**

Anthropologie Dos Lagos is the result of a research project into the re-imagination and re-vitalization of Anthropologie, the women's clothing and home furnishings store. Anthropologie wanted to modernize the brand, finding their current store design too cluttered with found objects, clothing, and goods. The proposal was twofold: first move the storage and display to perimeter walls; second use nature within the store to jolt consumers out of their normal mall experience.

In the Dos Lagos project, the façade is a crenellated "curtain" of cast-glass planks in a number of textures and finishes. This wiggling shape creates a series of display vitrines. Above this is a "green screen" with a series of holes in a gradient pattern that becomes more dense over the entrance. The screen will eventually be covered entirely with jasmine vines growing down from the roof. The entry awning is formed by a large aluminum folding door that closes off the store after hours.

Within the store are a series of display niches and new store fixtures, from industrial-style steel shelves to plug-in walls and ceilings. The niches are finished with materials not traditionally used in retailing, including Panelite panels, silk-screened cork, acoustic insulation, and oriented strand board.

The L-shaped plan creates two focal points within the space. One is a large glazed interior courtyard, open to the sky, with a green suburban lawn and an orange tree, harking back to the site's former life as an orange grove. In contrast to the lifelike nature of the courtyard, there is the "Shoppable Hill" containing a bench, space for hanging clothing, power outlets, potted plants, etc.

2

4 View of display niche
opposite Stairs to the interior
courtyard **Elizabeth Felicella**

4

Diane Von Furstenberg Studio Headquarters

New York, New York

1

The headquarters building for Diane von Furstenberg (DVF) Studio, a fashion design company, is a new six-story structure built behind two landmarked façades in New York City's Meatpacking District. The building houses the company's flagship store, a flexible showroom/event space, design and administrative offices for a staff of 150, an executive suite, and a private penthouse apartment.

The project's diverse program is unified through a singular iconic gesture: a stairway that collects and distributes light from the roof through to the deepest interior of the building. This shaft of light is conceived as an inhabitable and connective "stairdelier"—a cross between stair and chandelier—that cuts diagonally up from the ground floor to the "diamond," a faceted glass penthouse at the roof.

To maximize natural light, a series of heliostat mirrors are installed within the diamond. The primary mirror, facing south, tracks the sun throughout the day, reflecting it to a fixed secondary mirror that beams the sunlight down the stair, always at the same angle. Tertiary mirrors along the stair's length further direct the light onto the stair's guardrail—vertical steel cables that are structurally braced with Swarovski glass crystals. The crystals also help disperse the light to each floor.

The project is conceived as a dialogue between contemporary materials and renovated elements. The ground-floor façade is floor-to-ceiling panels of tempered glass set behind the existing cast-iron columns in order to emphasize the distinction between the new and old. Within, the store is designed as a wrap wall that winds its way diagonally across the ground floor and contains all the display fixtures.

A number of elements were assembled on-site. The diamond penthouse was built from solid steel members in Olot, Spain, shipped in containers to the US, and bolted together on site. The precast concrete stairdelier was lowered into the building by crane.

The building contains many sustainable elements, including geothermal heating and cooling via three 1,500-feet-deep wells. The stairdelier reduces the need for artificial light and is lit with energy-efficient LED lights at night. A green roof terrace at the sixth floor is planted with native grasses and wildflowers.

1 The executive space **2** DVF Studio headquarters from the southeast **3** The penthouse, from above **4** Night view **Elizabeth Felicella**

6

5

7

8

9

5 View from the penthouse to the terrace **6** The diamond penthouse at dusk **7** View of the stairdelier from the stage **8** View of the stairdelier from the offices **9** The DVF stairdelier: a cross between a staircase and a chandelier **Elizabeth Felicella**

Kew Gardens Hills Library

Queens, New York

This is an expansion and replacement of an existing library. The building is organized around a perimeter of open rooms for adults, teens, children, and staff. This band is capped with a green roof, completing a continuous "loop of green" with the building's side gardens.

The façade is a literal lifting up of the library's exterior walls to broadcast its activities to the outside. The apex is the main reading room at the most public corner, with a second "mini peak" at the children's room. Between these two peaks, the façade dips to provide privacy for the staff areas. This concrete beam is also structural, requiring only two columns along its length.

The exterior façade is made from GFRC in a curtain-like pattern of vertical folds. By folding a section of the façade over the street, much like one would mark one's place in a favorite book, an awning is created.

1

2

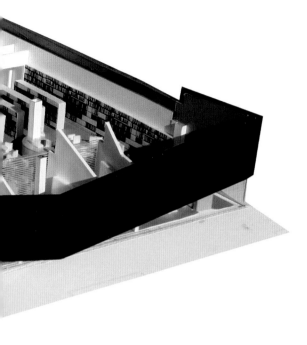

1 View of the model from northwest **2** View of the model from northeast **3** Day rendering of Kew Gardens Hills Library **4** Night rendering of library, with its lifted façade **WORKac**

4

3

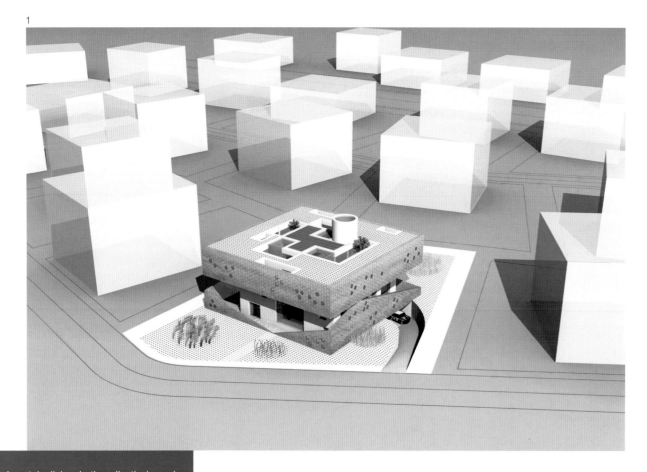

1

1 Bird's-eye-view of
Ordos **2** Exterior pool
3 View of the courtyard

ORDOS
Ordos, China

This house is an experiment in living both collectively and
individually. Given the harsh climate and crowded neighborhood,
it is focused on a complex interior world. The ground floor is the
"onion"—a series of perimeters expanding from structural walls
to circulation and from the pool and garden to the façade. In the
center is an enormous room that can be used for gatherings.
Openings focus views upward, rather than outward. The upper
floor is the "hutong"—a dense collection of rooms and courtyards
organized in four private quadrants, each independently accessed
via stairways. In the center is a small family living area that can
only be accessed through the outdoor courtyards.

2

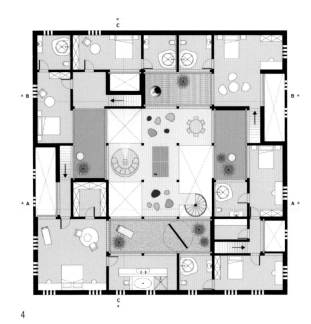

4

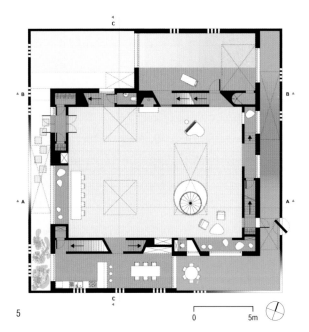

5

0   5m

6

4 Third floor plan **5** First floor plan **6** View of the living room **7** The large room at the rear of the house **WORKac**

7

P.F.1
P.S.1 Contemporary Art Center

Queens, New York

1 Folded farm over the courtyard wall **2** View of P.S.1 and P.F.1 **Elizabeth Felicella**

1

Since 1999, New York's Museum of Modern Art and its sister institution, the P.S.1 Contemporary Art Center, has hosted the Young Architects Program (YAP) to design a temporary installation in the courtyards of P.S.1 in Queens, New York for their summer "Warm Up" parties. In 2008, 40 years after the summer of 1968, it was time for a new leisure revolution, one that creates a new symbol of liberation, knowledge, power, and fun for today's cities. Leaving behind the Urban Beach, this project became the Urban Farm—as a symbol of our generation's preoccupation with and hopes for a better and different future.

Stemming from the desire to embrace the grid as an organizing pattern for the urban farm and working with structural material that had to be recyclable and biodegradable, cardboard tubes served as planters, preassembled in a "daisy" pattern of six tubes arranged in a hexagon around a seventh central tube. Fifty-one varieties of herbs, fruit, and vegetables were selected for their ability to thrive in an urban environment and planted strategically to bloom in succession throughout the summer.

P.F.1 is completely off-grid. The solar power system consists of an array of 18 photovoltaic modules to meet all of P.F.1's power loads—video screens, speakers, lights, cell phone chargers, and all irrigation pumps. A drip irrigation system was designed to deliver a controlled amount of water to each planter tube, fed by a cistern that collected more than 6,000 gallons of rainwater over the course of the summer.

Unbeknownst to MoMA, the proposed "tool shed" was actually a chicken coop! On the day of the opening six mature chickens and a dozen peeping chicks were brought in. The chickens had the run of the grounds during the week and produced eggs all summer long.

2

3

5

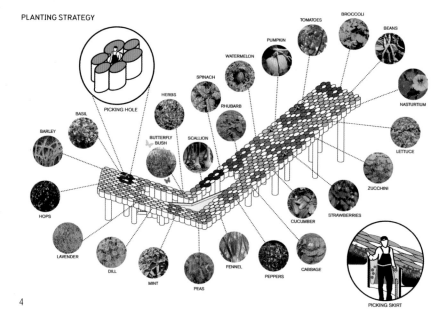

PLANTING STRATEGY

PICKING HOLE

BARLEY

BASIL

HERBS

SPINACH

RHUBARB

WATERMELON

PUMPKIN

TOMATOES

BROCCOLI

BEANS

NASTURTIUM

HOPS

BUTTERFLY
BUSH

SCALLION

LETTUCE

ZUCCHINI

LAVENDER

DILL

MINT

PEAS

FENNEL

PEPPERS

CABBAGE

CUCUMBER

STRAWBERRIES

PICKING SKIRT

4

3 Folded farm settles in the courtyard **4** Planting strategy **5** Daisy chaise **6** Daisy-pattern planting structure **7** Light and shade under the farm **8** View from the roof **Raymond Adams; Elizabeth Felicella; WORKac**

6

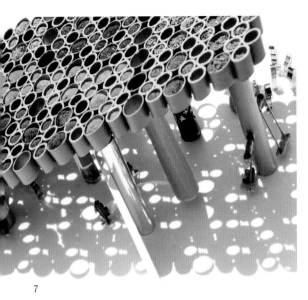

7

8

224 Centre Street, 5th Floor, New York, NY, 10013

WXY Architecture

www.wxystudio.com

CREATING FORMS/SPACES FOR SOCIAL INTERACTION.

WHO WE ARE:
Claire Weisz, Mark Yoes, Layng Pew

Staff 2010: Robert Berry, Christopher Kupski, Alan Tse, Yeju Choi, Kayt Brumder, Travis Eby, Maiko Shimizu, Chris Fox, Jenny Polak, Jo Lamont, Adriel Mesznik, Leah Solk, Shachi Pandey, Matthew Gilbert

OUR ARCHITECTURAL VALUES IN A DOZEN WORDS:
We value starting with constraints and ending by designing something uniquely resolved.

OUR ARCHITECTURAL PHILOSOPHY IN THREE-DOZEN WORDS:
Architecture's role is twofold: to make things better and tell it like it is. Architecture serves the clients' goals and the larger goals of the community with environmental, structural, and aesthetic integrity (clarity and self awareness).

WHY WE PRACTICE IN NEW YORK IN TWO-DOZEN WORDS:

NYC is the ultimate urban laboratory. We seek new territory for architecture, blurring boundaries between design scales, using the process to make positive change.

FREQUENT COLLABORATORS:
Buro Happold
Front
Piet Oudolf
West 8
Local Projects
Winterhouse
Doyle Design
Starr Whitehouse
MNLA
Jim Conti

OUR PRACTICE IN 20-DOZEN WORDS:

WXY Architecture was founded in 1998 as Weisz + Yoes when Claire Weisz and Mark Yoes created a base for their collaborative architectural vision. Early projects were formally ambitious with tight budget and time constraints. The results were small, inventive buildings, including the pavilion for the Museum of Jewish Heritage and The House in the Springs. Focusing on change in the public realm, the firm created public landscapes on challenging sites and urban design plans for re-imagining infrastructure. A recycling center and a new type of sanitation garage, along with designs for security booths and interactive information centers, expanded this focus. In 2009 the firm renamed itself WXY Architecture with the arrival of partner Layng Pew.

Much of WXY's work is about social and environmental transformation. Many commissions were initiated by the firm in collaboration with community, public, and private clients. Always deeply rooted in studies of the opportunities and limitations of the specific context, the firm's work articulates emerging hybrid programs that reflect the complexities of contemporary life and create new armatures for social interaction. WXY is interested in the precision of design and the experimental nature of all forms of building. The firm's recognition of the fundamentally cooperative and cross-disciplinary nature of contemporary design has sparked fruitful collaborations with new media designers, landscape designers, engineers, and visual artists, creating a rich palette and materiality, striking geometries, as well as the sometimes low-tech and other times cutting-edge sustainable technologies.

1

Battery Bosque/ SeaGlass Carousel
Battery Park, New York, New York

Once a 2-acre area of asphalt, the Bosque now fulfills historic Battery Park's potential as a destination. A design collaboration with Piet Oudolf and landscape architects Starr Whitehouse, this park—with spaces to sit, eat, and play—is a lushly planted porch to the vast acreage of New York's Inner Harbor.

The design's elements articulate the new curvilinear geometry of the park. The elliptical kiosks are derived from a series of arcs and made of certified sustainably harvested hardwood. The benches were designed to hold up to the punishing wear and tear of relaxing New Yorkers with an absolutely minimal use of material. Both kiosks and benches employ computer controlled manufacturing technology, giving the architects direct control over the fabrication of subtly differentiated multiples. A walk-through water feature based on the spiral of Archimedes anchors the northern end of the Bosque.

To complete the park's upgrade, there is also a sea-life themed carousel. The SeaGlass project transforms the traditional ride structure into an instrument of the future with digital projection and electrified glass technology known as Smart Glass.

SeaGlass's underwater theme references its location on the site of the first home of the New York Aquarium. The spiraling structure will be of stainless steel and glass, forming a shell whose interior provides a white screen for underwater projections. Using the paradigm of the magic lantern, the Smart Glass changes from clear to opaque as the ride begins, dimming the space in a rising sequence to capture the experience of diving under water.

The client's focus on design innovation has resulted in a park that is rich and colorful in its planting and playful in its architecture, a series of public spaces and features that respond to the site's extraordinary heritage with a contemporary sensibility.

1 Overview of the Bosque **2** Kiosk with bike rider **3** The fountain is designed so that visitors can walk through it **4** Site plan **Amy Barkow; WXY Architecture**

2

3

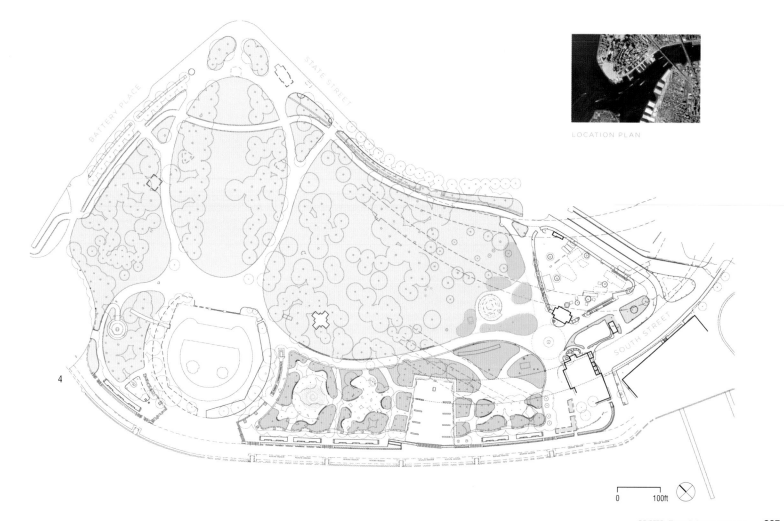

4

LOCATION PLAN

0   100ft

5

5 SeaGlass carousel at night 6 Carousel uses digital projection and advanced glass technology 7 Kiosk at night 8 Detail of bench **Amy Barkow; WXY Architecture**

6

7

8

Bronx Charter School
Hunts Point, Bronx, New York

This award-winning design for the Bronx Charter School for the Arts reflects the school's founding principle that arts education is critical to human development and learning. Color, space, and natural light create a direct physical connection with the content and aims of the curriculum. Through its adaptive re-use of an old factory, the school plays a role in the transformation of its industrial Hunts Point neighborhood. To achieve a healthy environment that enhances the learning spaces despite budget and site restrictions, a simple innovative approach was needed. A design process that involved the community and future teaching staff resulted in a unique, light-filled space that dovetails with Bronx Art's educational mission.

The use of a complex rhythm of brightly colored glazed brick for the façade contributes a strong street presence called for by the school's mission to promote community participation through the arts. Wide openings and minimal division of continuous space serve the founders' goal of using the built environment to encourage openness and communication. The classrooms are conceived as studio spaces. White and grey surfaces predominate to make the most of the north light, with color stripes providing orientation to each of the classroom bays, back towards the street, and the shared arts spaces along the façade.

Many low-cost sustainable features were incorporated and the building far exceeds the minimum standards for air changes, filtered fresh air, and in particular natural light both for productivity and to reduce lighting loads. The decision to reuse the façade structure (adding a new insulated brick layer) resulted in energy and material savings. Many of the materials used have a minimum of 80 percent recycled content. The long rows of north-facing skylights with insulated clerestories limit heat gain while bringing natural light into the classrooms and interior spaces of the former cold storage warehouse throughout the day.

1 Inviting façade opens up to street, with brightly colored glazed brick **2** Building sections **3** Plan **4** Classroom design maximizes daylight **5** Open learning spaces are full of light and air **Albert Vecerka/Esto**

1 Lobby
2 Second grade classroom
3 Kindergarten
4 Mezzanine
5 ESL
6 Fourth grade classroom
7 Multipurpose space

1 Kindergarten
2 First grade classroom
3 Second grade classroom
4 Third grade classroom
5 Fourth grade classroom
6 Multipurpose space
7 ESL

8 Lunch area
9 Parents' room
10 Music room
11 Dance/drama room
12 Gallery
13 Art room

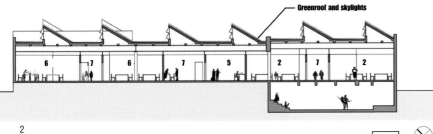

2

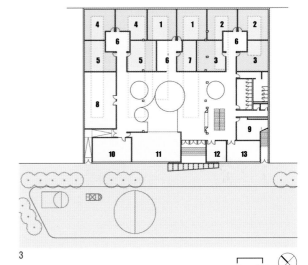

3

4

5

BRONX EMS 27
Bronx, New York

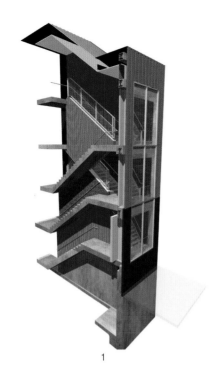

1

2

WXY was commissioned to design EMS 27 for the Fire Department of New York as a part of the Design Excellence Program of New York City's Department of Design and Construction. The facility will be the home base for six ambulance crews in the Northern Bronx. A custom exterior zinc panel system unfolds into sun control and privacy louvers to allow for light and views where needed. The complex program is accommodated in two interlocking blocks, using the limited footprint to maximum advantage. A double-height apparatus floor is overlooked by the office mezzanine, while the locker-room floor has a double-height connection to the penthouse lounge area. Linking these functions is a color-coded scissor stair that extends above the main roof to the penthouse lounge.

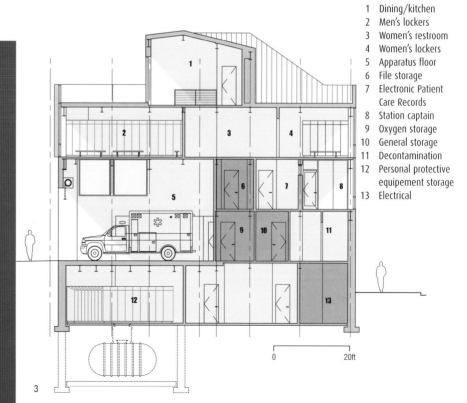

3

1 Dining/kitchen
2 Men's lockers
3 Women's restroom
4 Women's lockers
5 Apparatus floor
6 File storage
7 Electronic Patient Care Records
8 Station captain
9 Oxygen storage
10 General storage
11 Decontamination
12 Personal protective equipement storage
13 Electrical

0   20ft

4

1 Section through scissor stair and wall construction 2 View of station toward the southeast 3 Longitudinal section 4 Exterior zinc louvers are operable **WXY Architecture**

House in the Springs
Long Island, New York

1

The House in the Springs is located in an area well known to artists for its unique quality of light. It is a building designed to open up to the light and to the surrounding Long Island landscape. The clients, an arts lawyer and her developer husband, sought a country house with guest quarters and a place for themselves as well as a substantial open space, for less than $100 per square foot.

The project develops the geometry of a simple box stretched along its diagonal axis to make a three dimensional parallelogram whose constituent triangles appear to slide past each other, pivoting upwards. As a result, the house seems to pull the landscape into its interior space, so that the occupants feel as though they are part of the landscape. Porches completely surround the house, resolving the parallelogram geometry, and creating uniquely shaped spaces that frame the landscape from the interior.

Emphasizing the diagonal axis, the roof is held up by three great plywood bents or beam-and-column systems of laminated wood, a structure that allows great flexibility in the placement of interior walls. Adding to the fluidity of the interior spaces, the different ceiling heights of the guest spaces and the master bedroom create an opportunity for a dynamic ramp that overlooks the light-filled double-height living room.

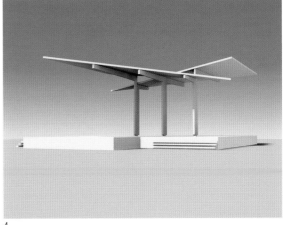

1 Exterior, showing guest room **2** Exterior, from afar **3** Exterior, porch **4** Concept rendering
Paul Warchol Photography

5

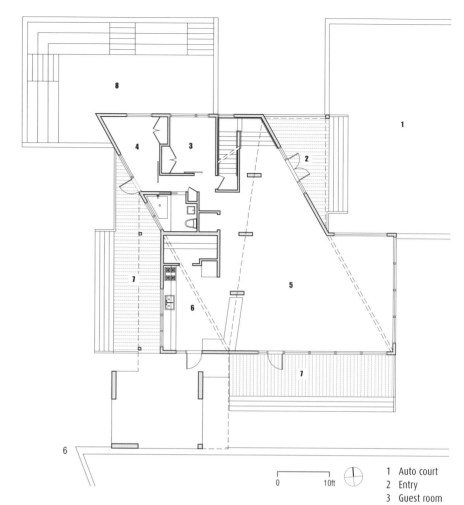

8

1

4   3

2

7

5

6

7

6

0   10ft

1   Auto court
2   Entry
3   Guest room
4   Office
5   Living/dining
6   Kitchen
7   Deck
8   Sunken patio

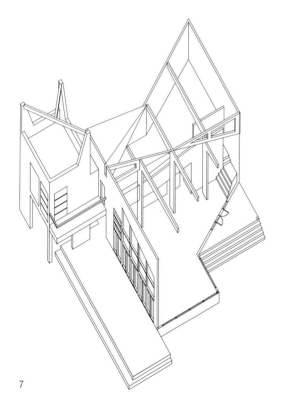

7

8

5 Ground floor interior, showing bents **6** Ground floor plan **7** Axonometric plan **8** Interior ramp/gallery
9 Interior living space **Paul Warchol Photography**

Monsignor John J. Kowsky Plaza

Battery Park City, New York, New York

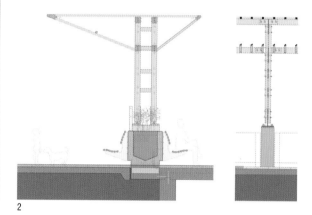

1 The structure provides shading and an armature for vines **2** Typical section **3** Site plan and section **4** In context with Cesar Pelli's World Financial Center **following pages** Vines take over the structure **A. Vecerka/ESTO**

Located over the original World Trade Center pump house, this new public space overlooks the Hudson River and connects Liberty Street to the river esplanade. Its amenities include a shaded plaza, a play area for younger children, and a dog run. The project was technically challenging as access to the pumps beneath had to be maintained in the completed design. The project also reconceived areas below the overlook, to knit the raised plaza into the esplanade along the Hudson River.

A cantilevered shade structure more than 300 feet long defines the space. The Ipe wood trellis is detailed with stainless steel cable and fittings. Its balancing and articulation reflect the lack of solid ground, the result of the pumping infrastructure beneath. Precast concrete planters carry flame vine and wisteria, which create a deeply planted arbor, evolving into a new green space. The structure is unique in that there is no redundancy between the stainless steel and the Ipe wood frame: all parts are playing structural roles. The structure offers shade throughout the day. Buro Happold was the collaborating engineering firm on this project, which was awarded a 2008 AIA New York State Award of Merit.

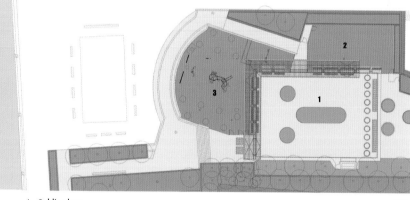

1 Public plaza
2 Dog run
3 Playground
4 Hudson River

0   50ft

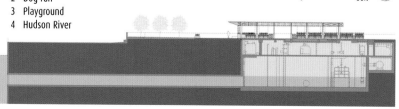

4

Surf Avenue Bridge
Brooklyn, New York

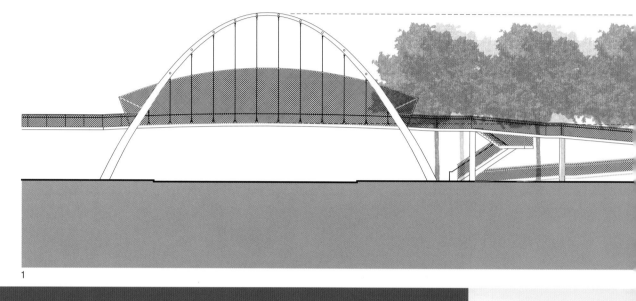

1

Coney Island, New York City's iconic stretch of urban seaside, has a reputation as the birthplace of American pop culture. This has prompted a wave of new plans for Coney Island's attractions and public spaces. Among the initial investments were a refurbishment of the Parachute Jump, a new solar subway station, and work on two elevated subways by prominent conceptual artists.

WXY was commissioned to design the proposed new pedestrian bridge and pedestrian causeway spanning Surf Avenue at West Eighth Street to connect the West8/Aquarium BMT subway station to the Boardwalk. The bridge and causeway is a signature structure reflecting new opportunities for the Coney Island entertainment district and the ambitious plans of the nearby New York Aquarium. The design, commissioned by the New York City Department of Design and Construction under the Design Excellence program, has received broad public support, and forms a part of plans for the overall development of the district.

For pedestrian safety, the bridge required restrictive enclosure systems and the design incorporates these constraints to create a fluent structure that relates to the language of the famous Cyclone roller coaster close by. The tubular parabolic bridge launches itself across Surf Avenue—becoming the main path for community access to the aquarium and the beach, as well as a new formal and iconic marker signaling the location of the aquarium.

2

Labels on elevation:
¢ Arch Apex + 60'-0"
T.O. Bridge Deck + 20'-8"
Sidewalk + 0'-0"

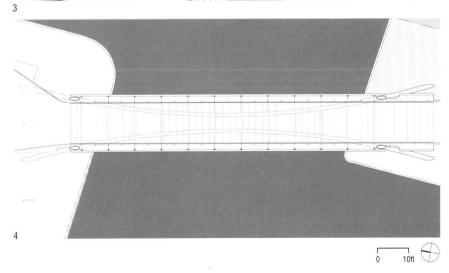

3

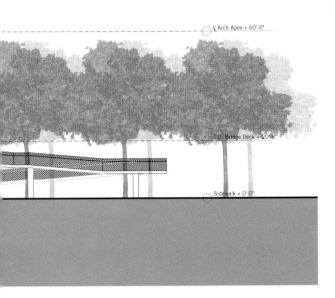

4

0   10ft

1 Elevation **2** The form of the bridge was inspired by a nearby roller coaster **3** The bridge connects a causeway to the subway station **4** Plan **WXY Architecture**

Zipper Bench
New York City Parks Department, New York

The Zipper Bench is part of a series of park elements created as part of a commission to redesign New York City's standard issue park benches. These key elements in the city's civic vocabulary date back to the World's Fairs of 1939 and 1964. WXY created a new system of park elements with highly flexible functionality. The new benches had to withstand wear and tear from the millions of visitors to New York City's park system. Principles of sustainability were a priority as the firm reconsidered each of the basic park elements against its historic type. The new designs are made of powder-coated steel. They use less material than their predecessors, and no hardwood.

To reinvent the classic New York park bench as a system suited to the curvilinear geometry of contemporary park design the architect turned to computer-driven CNC bending technology. This not only facilitates the ergonomic shaping of the bench slats but also allows differentiated multiples to be created economically. Taking full advantage of the technology, a set of modular variations that could be tailored to the specific conditions of each varied park site was developed.

Versions of the bench include double-sided, backless, and armless pieces. Echoing the form of its namesake, the design's iterations may be combined such that the "front" and "back" of a double-sided bench part and flow seamlessly into two divergent shapes. The fluid transition from one form to another gives the bench a sculptural quality that can influence and inspire the surrounding landscape.

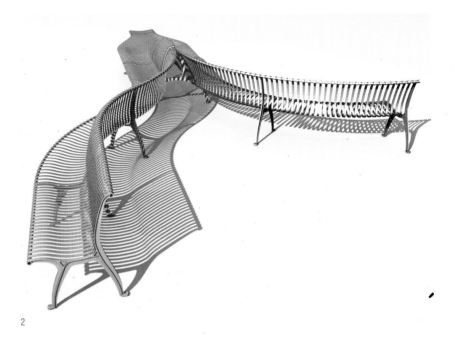

1 The Zipper Bench lays down and undulates up 2 Rendering
3 The Zipper Bench intersects with a tree **Ken Taranto**

Acknowledgments

Many people contributed to the realization of this book. First and foremost are Alessina Brooks and Paul Latham of The Images Publishing Group, who instigated the idea of a revisit of the New York Five, in search of a new generation, the New York Dozen. Their support and encouragement of this book is valued, as is their friendship and collaboration over the past 20 years.

To Kristen Richards, a friend and colleague, I am indebted not only for her insightful foreword, but also for her suggestions, leads, and counsel in selecting the architects of the New York Dozen.

Others were generous with their time, recollections, and assessments of architecture then and now. I wish to thank Peter Eisenman, Michal Graves, Charles Gwathmey, and Richard Meier for talking to me about the heady days of the New York Five. John Hejduk's wife, Gloria, and his daughter, Renate, lent insight into Hejduk's place within the New York Five. Paul Goldberger provided a great sense of what was happening in New York and the larger architectural stage during the 1970s, and the legacy of the Five. Suzanne Stephens shared some wonderful stories regarding the escalation of the war between the Grays and the Whites, as did Robert A.M. Stern, whose writings on the period were invaluable. I am indebted to Beverly Willis for her insights into the young practitioners of New York.

Without the New York Dozen, of course, this book wouldn't be. I want to thank not only the New York architects who contributed their work and a sense of themselves to this book, but also their staff, photographers, and others involved in the machinations of project documentation, and their prompt responses to myriad requests.

I also wish to thank colleagues who critiqued the text, suggested architects to consider, or assisted in research, including Dariel Cobb, Dhiru Thadani, Mary Bishop Coan, and Jen Schaefer.

Michael J. Crosbie